The Bible:
Fact, Fiction, Fantasy, Faith

The Bible:
Fact, Fiction, Fantasy, Faith

Hubert N. Dukes

Foreward by Robert C. Kimball

Lancaster–Miller Publishers

Copyright © 1981 Hubert N. Dukes

Lancaster-Miller Publishers
3165 Adeline Street
Berkeley, California 94703

ISBN 0-89581-040-9

Library of Congress No. 81-17169

Editor and Designer: Nancy Grimley Carleton
Typesetter: Tayloe Typesetting
Printer: Braun-Brumfield, Inc.

Printed and bound in the United States of America.

I want to express my appreciation to my wife Dorothy and to the other members of my family who gave me their encouragement over years of preparation and to other friends too numerous to list who encouraged me in the publication of this book. I also wish to express my gratitude to two friends who helped me greatly with their pointed questions and suggestions as to the development of my ideas and the structure of my writing—Dr. Paul Kirkpatrick, retired from the Stanford faculty, and Karl Schwenke, a writer friend of Wells River, Vermont. Others who helped me greatly were Maxine MacDonald who read critically the final draft and Jean Garrett who spent hours typing the corrected manuscript. My deep appreciation goes also to Nancy Carleton of Lancaster-Miller for her careful attention to the details of the publication.

Contents

Foreward

I first met Hubert Dukes over twenty years ago. He was at that time minister of the Congregational Church in north Berkeley. North Church, known as the friendly family church, was an interesting blend of a predominantly conservative social temperament with a healthy liberal component. During the sixties, controversial issues such as the Fair Housing Ordinance and the Vietnam War sometimes threatened to tear our church apart. Hubert's depth as a preacher constantly offered perspective on the human needs and wants of our times. His personal caring, along with that of his wife Dorothy, built bridges where impossible gorges seemed to divide.

Meeting Hubert in 1960 brought, among other things, the thrill of coming across one of the great preachers and pastors of our times—a man of unusually clear integrity, wisdom, wit, and compassion. For years, Hubert held us together: marrying, burying, playing bridge, calling on the rich, poor and in-between, and all the time maintaining that steady beat of his preaching and the tempo of the Gospel to which he was alert.

Since his retirement from full-time ministering to one congregation, a group from North Church has followed Hubert about the land. If Hubert preaches, the group goes. We still hold periodic dinners and seminars on the state of the Union. Knowing Hubert is also knowing Dorothy. She matches him in acumen and conversational strength. If there is touching, sanity, equality, intimacy in

9

the institution of marriage, Dorothy and Hubert model it for all who know them. Through his own example and through the guidance he offers others, Hubert's ministering continues.

With the shift from full-time preaching, Hubert began to devote more of his energy to writing. This book is the primary fruit of that effort. As usual, Hubert's scholarship is wondrous. He cuts through pedantics to wisdom (having worked intimately with theological faculties for twenty-five years, I know how uncommon is this capacity). Through this book, Hubert's vision of the guiding Spirit behind the Bible reaches out to even more people than his ministry has already touched.

This book is especially important because we are living in a time of more and more references to the Bible coming out of a conservative or fundamentalist orientation. Some of these conservative and fundamentalist Christians may be trained in higher critical scholarship of the Scriptures, but they rarely allow such training to interfere with their literalistic mentality for moralizing. In contrast, Hubert's passionate understanding allows the Judeo-Christian heritage, especially as gathered in the Bible, to speak to our age. Today, as in all times, the need for this quality of learning is great.

The Scriptures address matters of justice, love, and freedom of the spirit. Having been lovingly raised in the heart of the Georgia Bible Belt, Hubert understands such a persuasion but also realizes that these concerns can be distorted to the level of mere laws, even laws controlling loving and the curtailment of the Spirit. Hubert's interpretation of the Bible from a historical perspective shows us how we can best translate its teachings into our own lives.

Hubert says this book is written for the ordinary church layperson. I disagree. Leadership and laity both can learn from it. In his exposition on the Book of Proverbs, Hubert suggests some literary similarities to colonial American writing such as Franklin's *Poor Richard's Almanack* or Emerson's *Essays*. Then he adds:

> These proverbs of a people often seem a better guide to their fundamental character than theology. Theologies are subject to radical change, and then they cause bitter strife. Contemporary history shows that theology has too often led to conflict and wars. But human nature and human behavior do not change radically or vary from race to race. The proverbs of humanity could furnish a ground for better understanding and peace between nations. How much pain might humanity have been spared if we had heeded the lesson "Pride goeth before destruction...Before honor is humility."

In this book, Hubert unfolds the substance of the Bible, the development of the Bible, and the relevance of the Bible. Praise and thanks be to him.

Robert C. Kimball
Professor of Theology, Graduate Theological Union
President, Thomas Starr King School for Religious Leadership
Berkeley, California

Introduction

What? Another book about the Bible? What good will it do? I myself once asked that question. I found that the struggle with the question has created my answer. Still—we must start with the question. After all, many people claim, "No one reads the Bible anymore." Yet the Bible remains a continual best-seller—a fact which would seem to contradict these skeptics. So a second claim is raised: "But people don't really read it!" A variation on this statement was recently made by Leo Rosten in a comment in *Saturday Review*. He wrote, "It always astonishes me to learn how little even religious folks know about the Bible. I am no less unhinged by how little agnostics know."

Most people are not completely ignorant about the Bible. Many are able to quote well-known and appealing bits from the Scriptures. But when questioned, these same people can't tell you whether the quotation really comes from the Bible; for all they know it could be from Shakespeare or *Poor Richard's Almanack*.

Those who attend church, of course, do hear the Bible read in its full variety. From personal experience I know that passages from the Bible are read, Sunday after Sunday, from innumerable pulpits. But I also know—likewise from personal experience—that the people who hear these lessons are as puzzled by them as they are by the figures on economic growth; in both cases it's impossible for people to figure out what it all means *to them*. So they clutch at the first explanation that is offered them—even if it's avowedly

13

sectarian. Such personal, sectarian interpretations have divided adherents of the Bible with a bitterness that often results in bloody wars—not only in past times, but even in our own day. Look, for example, at Northern Ireland; look at Lebanon; look at the Middle East.

Just as such wars have proven to be futile in resolving disagreements over the Bible, so has the naive assumption that dogma, doctrine, or meaningful historical interpretations can be created out of selected biblical statements. Yet history has also been replete with this form of tragic dogmatic assertiveness. On a personal level, we all know someone who claims to prove his point of view about modern life and morals, or who claims to know God's true feelings about other people's behavior patterns, through some simplistic biblical quotes.

Recently, during a debate in the California legislature, one representative read from the Bible an ancient law advocating death for sexual deviates. The legislator did not advocate importing such a punishment into the twentieth century, but he felt the passage did give him "a sacred duty" to support stiff penalties toward homosexuals. He didn't dare read the entire passage, however, for there he would also have found a law advocating the stoning to death of rebellious sons—and he wasn't quite ready to support *that* biblical "duty."

The Bible exists within a historical matrix, and to ignore that matrix is to court disaster (or, as in the case of the California legislator, ridicule). Yet ignore it we have. This selective blindness has fostered divisions in our country and has eroded the tolerance of others necessary to sustain our democratic processses—for without tolerance we could never settle the difficult issues that separate us. At one time unions were considered "organs of Satan"—so there was violence. Now they are accepted parts of our economy, welcomed as a steadying force even by the big manufacturers who once found the very idea intolerable. A similar blindness has enabled people to find justification for their irrational persecution of Jews, blacks, Chicanos, and any other group that has felt the sting of prejudice.

While there are some who profess to understand the Bible (though they ignore its historical background), most people just complain that they cannot understand it at all. The latter are often well-educated in other areas, yet they "cop out" about the Bible by saying, "It's too deep for me." This need not be true. Any reasonably intelligent person willing to invest a bit of time can understand the basic structure of the Bible. This doesn't mean becoming scholars—few of us are or should be. Most biblical scholars spend their whole lives studying small segments of the Bible. They don't presume to know all there is to know.

In the first place, the serious biblical scholar knows that he is doomed to ignorance about many crucial matters. The writings are old and have been patch-worked together over centuries and by different cultures. While a great deal is known about these ancient cultures, much still waits to be discovered—and much never will be. But one does not need a scholar's knowledge or dedication to comprehend the nature of the Bible, in its individual books or as an entity.

I have written this book in order to assist those of you who are interested in the Bible, but who have only a meager background to rely on. Maybe you were dragged to church every week; maybe you crammed for a Bar Mitzvah or First Communion. But you rebelled against such force-feeding, and only now are you becoming interested in the Bible of your own free will, out of curiosity or renewed conviction. For you, I have written this guide.

My basic argument is a simple one. In order to gain a comprehension of the nature of the Bible, we must ask four questions of any verse, passage, or book: Who wrote it? When was it written? For whom was it written? What was the goal the writer had in mind? These questions help us to put each book of the Bible in the context of its time. Only then can we truly understand the writings and judge their contemporary value. Secondly, this kind of examination can supplement the knowledge of parents who face their children's questions. It is high time that the vital background knowledge about biblical times and beliefs (now restricted to pastors, professors, and full-time students of the Bible) be shared with laypeople in a simple and honest way. Lastly, I have attempted to be objective. You will find here none of those sectarian theological presuppositions which mark so many books interpreting the Bible.

So far I have addressed two important questions about reading the Bible. But there remains a third, more pernicious than any other. There are those who ask, "Just why should I read the Bible at all?" They ask this question particularly if they have been told that the Bible is not infallible—not true from cover to cover. "If it's not true, it can't really be God's word," they say. "So why bother?"

In response to the above question, I would answer: The Bible is a library of books. Most of it *is* divinely inspired; but even the portions that are not are still the work of great minds speaking what their faiths told them were words of truth for themselves and for all mankind. Some of these writers felt that God had spoken directly to them. Others shared the faith of the great philosopher Spinoza (1632–1677) that reason can never be opposed to God's word, so that as they searched for the highest wisdom, they searched for the wisdom of God. The great leaders of past centuries have had their deeper emotions stirred and their sense of justice quickened by the thoughts of biblical writers—even if they didn't believe that their interpretations were the only truth.

There is much in the Bible you *don't* have to read— endless genealogies and outworn laws—except for the purpose of research. But woven through the stories and parables, the lives of prophets and saints, there are unchanging insights into life and the inspiration for a humane way of living. The persons of the Bible faced the mystery and wonder of the unknown, and from it they wrested a faith that carried them triumphantly through troubles and tragedies, and allowed them to face the unknown future with serene courage.

The Bible is not itself history, but is set in the midst of history. Reading it, you can watch ancient people fight their way through doubt and despair to build a nobler life for all humanity. Through its chronicles we can learn from the past, not repeat it.

Samuel Foss, in part of his poem "The Higher Catechism" [found in *The World's Great Religious Poetry* (New York: Macmillan, 1934)], has voiced the idea that we all share in the writing of the Bible. He asks:

> What is the word's true Bible?—
> 'Tis the highest thought of man,
> The thought distilled through ages,
> Since the dawn of thought began.
> And each age adds a thought thereto,
> Some Psalm or promise sweet—
> And the canon is unfinished,
> And forever incomplete.
> O'er the chapters that are written
> Long and lovingly we pore—
> But the best is yet unwritten,
> For we grow from more to more.

The purpose of this book, then, is to make the Bible as it has been written over the long ages understandable to persons of this day. Through understanding past struggles of faith, we, who struggle with the same problems in our day, may be helped in our tasks.

To speak of the Bible in terms of fact, fiction, fantasy, and faith does not disparage either its historic *or* its religious value. Nor does it hinder our ability to see the tales of the Bible as part of historic situations. History is supported by facts, but no history claims to be completely factual. In historic writings fiction must be mixed with the facts. Every history is inevitably a single person's vision of the past, an imagined reconstruction—not the past itself. Likewise, myths generally underlie the often fantastic faiths people use to uphold this nation's virtues or preserve its traditions about heroes. Is Johnny Appleseed a fact? Fact, fiction, fantasy, and myth are all fused in any work concerning the past. Moreover, in religion fiction helps to illuminate great truths by providing specific examples instead of difficult abstractions. Fantasy gives wings to human hope in the most desperate of times; myths are vehicles to voice faiths that transcend reason, but are true nevertheless.

In service of that truth, I have tried to avoid an undue number of the theological formulas of contemporary religions that have developed based on the Bible. The various preachers of these formulas have in turn appealed to the Bible to support them; but, since I am purposely analyzing the writings of the Bible as an objective commentator, I want to avoid any possibility of appealing to one group at the expense of another. In any case, I feel that we can best comprehend the Bible by looking at the historical movements which preceded the theological interpretations: You must know what you're talking about first; then you can concentrate on your individual position.

For the sake of clarity and conciseness, I have not tried to offer detailed citations for all the statements I have made, even though many of them sound different from the catchy statements about the Bible you may have heard expressed with more heat than light. Long footnotes have their place, but this book is not one of them. I have, however, listed in the bibliography a number of books by eminent Jewish and Christian scholars that are available in any good library. Anyone who desires more details—and my goal will be achieved if you finish this book saying, "I want more"— can find in them much that I have had to omit. I do not offer you "all of creation while standing on one foot"—I invite you to begin Everyman's journey.

Hubert N. Dukes
Palo Alto, California

Historical Summary

Long before the time of written records, in the second millennium B.C., a small group of Semitic people settled in Egypt. We know nothing about these people beyond their legends, which were gathered in what we now call the Old Testament hundreds of years after the Hebrews had left Egypt. The legends of their early history—before their arrival in Egypt—are contained in the Book of Genesis. According to the story, the early Hebrews were farmers and shepherds. During times of famine they were accustomed to migrating into Egypt where the Nile yielded water even during droughts. After one of these migrations, they were enslaved by the Egyptians; their captivity lasted some four centuries. They finally escaped from Egypt under the leadership of Moses, as narrated in the Book of Exodus. This Exodus is commonly taken to be the beginning of Hebrew history.

After living for some years in the wilderness lands that lie between Egypt and the land of Canaan (probably the Sinai and Negev deserts), the Hebrew people gained a foothold in the land that tradition asserted had been promised to them centuries before by their God, Yahweh. After several hundred years of wars and treaties they succeeded in becoming the dominant power in Canaan. Around 1000 B.C., they established a strong kingdom under their great king, David. The legends of the struggle to conquer this "Promised Land" are found in the books of Joshua and Judges; the sequence of events following their successful conquest is described in the books of Samuel and Kings.

There followed a comparatively brief period of wealth and power under King David and his son, Solomon. But, as a result of revolts by various factions and theological schisms, the kingdom fell apart less than a century after its establishment. This resulted in the creation of two kingdoms, one in the North known as Israel and another in the South known as Judea, whose rivalry for hegemony over the Hebrews weakened both realms.

Thus the two kingdoms fell to foreign invaders. The northern kingdom fell to the Assyrians in 721 B.C. The leaders were executed, and the people were taken into exile. Forced into exile, scattered, and denied religious services, these tribes were never heard from again. The legends of "the lost tribes of Israel" stem from this brutal act of conquest. The southern kingdom fell to the Babylonians in 586 B.C., and its inhabitants were sent into exile in Babylon. But the Babylonians allowed the Judeans to remain together, and even allowed them to return home in 538 B.C. (after capture by Cyrus the Persian). They rebuilt the city of Jerusalem and sought to re-establish the nation and its religion. But this nation, a tributary to its generous conquerors, was never very strong. It soon fell once more, this time to the Romans and was made a province of the empire. A final revolt against the Romans in A.D. 70 led to the final destruction of Israel. The story of the decline of the Hebrews can be found in the books of the prophets; the portrait of their beaten spirit is painted in Ecclesiastes and the so-called Wisdom Books of the Apocrypha.

Chronology

This is a brief chronology of biblical events and writings referred to in this book. Many of the dates are approximations.

ABRAHAM lived approximately around the period of 1800 B.C.

MOSES led the Exodus from Egypt around 1250 B.C.

INVASION and CONQUEST of the Promised Land occurred from approximately 1250 to 900 B.C.

SAUL reigned about 1028 B.C.

DAVID reigned from 1016 to 976 B.C.

SOLOMON reigned from 976 to 936 B.C. (Following Solomon's reign the kingdom was divided.)

FALL of the northern kingdom to the Assyrians took place in 721 B.C.

The EIGHTH CENTURY B.C. PROPHETS were active during approximately these periods:

    AMOS, 760–757 B.C.

    HOSEA, 745–735 B.C.

    MICAH, 735–721 B.C.

    ISAIAH, 740–700 B.C. (Writings attributed to Isaiah were actually the work of at least three people. His prophecies were added to after his death, probably around 540 B.C.)

The BOOK OF DEUTERONOMY was presumably discovered in the temple around 721 B.C.

JEREMIAH, 626–586 B.C.

EZEKIEL, 592–570 B.C.

FALL OF JERUSALEM. The destruction of the city took place in 586 B.C. This event marked the beginning of the seventy year exile of the leaders to Babylon.

RETURN of the exiles, 538 B.C.

LATER PROPHETS:

MALACHI, 475 B.C.

NEHEMIAH, 444 B.C.

EZRA, 397 B.C.

JONAH, 400 B.C.

PENTATEUCH finished around 350 B.C.

PROVERBS, 300–200 B.C.

DANIEL, 165 B.C.

ECCLESIASTES, 200–150 B.C.

PSALMS, about 150 B.C.

NEW TESTAMENT:

PAUL wrote approximately A.D. 50–65.

MARK'S GOSPEL was written after A.D. 70.

MATTHEW, A.D. 80–100.

LUKE and ACTS, possibly around A.D. 90.

The GOSPEL OF JOHN, probably after A.D. 100.

The Interpretation of Scripture

by Benedict De Spinoza

The masses take no pains at all to live according to the Scripture, and we see most people endeavoring to hawk about their own commentaries as the Word of God, and giving their best efforts, under the guise of religion, to compelling others to think as they do: we generally see, I say, theologians anxious to learn how to wring their inventions and sayings out of the sacred text, and to fortify them with Divine authority.... But if men really believed what they verbally testify of Scripture, they would adopt quite a different plan of life: their minds would not be agitated by so many contentions, nor so many hatreds, and they would cease to be excited by such a blind and rash passion for interpreting the sacred writings.... Ambition and unscrupulousness have waxed so powerful, that religion is thought to consist, not so much in respecting the writings of the Holy Ghost, as in defending human commentaries.[1]

1

From Cover to Cover

When I was a boy I lived in Georgia in the heart of the Bible Belt. The Church and the Bible were the focus of our community. In every home, in plain view on the living room table, lay an open Bible—just in case the preacher called. When he arrived, his first act would be to read from its pages and lead the family in prayer.

The Bible was revered as the word of God, "true from cover to cover." If anyone doubted, he was wise to keep it to himself, or be ostracized from the company of respectable folks. Since it was considered God's own words, the Bible was used as a final authority in any discussion, whether about religious doctrine, personal morals, or even political questions.

However, this faith in an infallible authority did not remove all conflicts from our community—even among the deeply religious people of my little town. If everyday life was rendered easier than in the "cities of the plain," the life of the spirit was far more hectic. We all agreed that the Bible was God's word, but we could never agree on what certain of those words *meant*. We all attended church, but on any given street each family might attend a different church and be fiercely loyal to its doctrines. There were significant differences between the various bodies of Christians, but each group could marshal up supporting verses of Scripture to back up its contentions. We could, and did, use

God's words against God's words.

From a distance some of my community's controversial issues may seem trivial, but to us they were accorded most serious consideration. The "wrong" method of baptism, for instance, could bring down eternal damnation! Some strongly contended it was necessary to be totally immersed in water after reaching adulthood; others were equally adamant that having a few drops sprinkled on their heads, even just after birth, was the only way. Each of these positions had the support of Scripture. These arguments over the differing forms of baptism led to estrangement between otherwise friendly neighbors. Often we could disguise our depth of feeling by indulging in a protective and sometimes silly banter over the matter. There were other times, however, when the matter created religious upheavals throughout our community.

Traveling evangelists were the rabble-rousers who brought these upheavals. Eager for converts, they espoused vicious dogmatic certainties over the question of baptism. They stirred up the community with their hostility, so that rival pastors would find themselves defending their positions for weeks, to the detriment of their normal spiritual duties.

All this came about because the churches of my childhood community were overwhelmingly concerned with salvation—with having the right faith to enter heaven. The first question we asked when a neighbor died was, "Had he accepted Jesus?" During revival meetings, lay workers would pursue the members of the congregation and ask, "Are you saved?" An ambiguous response led to further, persistent probing, for not to know was to be "lost" in a limbo that led to damnation.

Thus while the Scriptures were considered to be an infallible guide, there remained profound disagreements as to what else was required for salvation. The generally accepted view was that a person was saved by two things: faith in Jesus, as the Son of God, and belief in his sacrifice for sinners. It seemed strange to me then as it does even now that God would demand the death of his Son in order to forgive sinners. But as we will see, the Bible comes out of a harsher time when only death could redeem another death. Compared to this awful sacrifice, belief in the miracle of Jesus' birth was easy.

The doctrine of salvation was so strong that many were tempted to believe that it really didn't matter what a person did or how he behaved, if he only accepted Jesus. A popular spiritual seemed to sum it all up: "Jesus paid it all, all to him I owe." As a converse, they held that those who had never heard of Jesus, people in so-called heathen lands, were damned without a hearing—lost without ever knowing the rules of the contest.

There were exceptions, of course. Some radicals contended that what a person did, and how he lived, also mattered. This minority was accused of believing in salvation by works, one step away from the damned atheistical humanists. Some of the mainline salvationist churches went to the other extreme; they supported the salvation of the "elect." According to this rigid prescription, God has chosen a certain number to be saved. The others would be lost, no matter how saintly they were. The doctrine found support in Paul's writings (Romans 9) and in the writings of John Calvin. To me, the doctrine implies that those who are not of the elect can, so far as God is concerned, go to hell.

The point is that all these believers were able to find statements in the "infallible" Bible to uphold their various views. Referring to the consequent proliferation of views, J. Kenneth Galbraith wrote an essay in the book *A Contemporary Guide to Economy, Peace and Laughter* (Houghton-Mifflin, 1971) in which he stated:

> The contradiction of the New Testament also means that with a little effort anyone can find a faith that accords with his preferences, and can find a faith that accords to his tastes, even if fairly depraved. In consequence, dissidents are not excluded from the faith;

they are retained and accommodated in a different chapter.

Each of these views is still held by some church group—at least each is preserved in statements of faith or in liturgy. But I know now, from frequent visits to the churches of my youth, that there have been changes. The messages from today's pulpits are *not* the same. Today, people lack this strong faith in the infallibility of the Bible. Moreover, other controversies now preoccupy members of these southern churches, controversies involving human rights arising out of past injustices and deep uncertainties concerning education and the integration of the races.

As a rule the churches of my birthplace no longer cite the Bible with the same certainty as before because the questions they face are too deeply mixed up with customs, mores and legal statutes. Complex problems do not align with the seemingly simple answers found in holy writ. People still speak of the Bible as the word of God, but they are increasingly confused as to what that means. Their quandary has been described by Dr. James D. Smart, who writes:

> The Christian in the pew who listens to the reading of the Bible week by week is as mystified and confused as ever by these ancient and distant texts, until the constant reinforcement of his frustration leads him to conclude that the Bible is after all an incomprehensible and not very useful book.[2]

Of greater significance at the present time are the newer churches, which trace their history not to the first Protestant Revolution but to the Evangelical movements of the past two centuries. Faced with the lack of certainty on the part of the older established churches, members of these newer churches uphold the doctrine of the Infallibility of the Scriptures. They even call themselves "Bible churches."

My contact with the missionaries of these Bible churches has led me to conclude that they know only those parts of the Bible which buttress their prophecies of doom. Relying upon the books of Daniel and Revelation, they pronounce God's judgment upon the fallen world of the present. They assert that the Bible reveals no faith in man-made governments or in gradual reform. Only God, they contend, can save the world; luckily, his return is imminent. He will come soon, and he will descend with destructive fury upon his enemies. The millennium will have arrived.

The peril of this dogmatism is that Bible churches appeal not only to committed believers in the Bible but also to many persons, young and old, who are confused about present conditions in the world and who are looking for some certain cure or direct word from an authoritative source. These desperate seekers are led to believe that the Bible is an oracle, timeless in its nature and miraculous in its origin.

But the Bible is not an infallible oracle. What then, you might well ask, is it? Seen in its historic context, the Bible is a collection of writings produced by many writers living in widely differing circumstances over a long period of time. Dr. James Moffatt, the translator of a modern version of the Bible, has said of the New Testament authors, "They wrote for their own age, *without a thought for posterity* [my italics]." The writers of the Bible were concerned with their own problems. They had no intention of establishing God's word for future centuries. They were concerned solely with the vital issues of their own times.

These issues, of course, include some questions which face almost every people in history. The people of biblical times were confronted with many of the problems that face us today. They too confronted religious differences, racial animosity, intertribal bitterness, war, and struggles for power. Their writings, like our churches, reflect widely differing concepts of God.

There is in these writings, for example, the reflection of a primitive animism—gods conceived as spirits or powers revealed in natural manifestations. Rivers flood because the river gods are angry; crops flourish because the earth gods are happy. Angels are messengers of the gods. To the Hebrews, God lived on Mount Sinai. His voice was heard in the thunder, and his presence was manifested in the lightning. From his presence the people recoiled in fear. How well I recall my own fear, when I heard my father read the account in the nineteenth chapter of Exodus describing God's appearance to Moses!

Later, the Hebrew God became a tribal God. Later still, he was the God of the Hebrew nation, leading the army into battle against those who worshipped other gods. It was not until centuries had passed that he became the universal God of love and justice.

These historical changes in the portrayal of God cause difficulty, especially for the casual reader of the Bible. Some readers are particularly disturbed by the cruelty condoned by the Old Testament God. A friend whose perception I admire once wrote to me, disconsolate, "Reading from the Bible is a chore for me. I am repelled by the contradictions, the cruelty, murders and horrors, the assassination of men, women and children." He went on to plead for someone to compile a Bible without the horrors that couldn't possibly be the word of *his* God.

What my friend suggested has been done occasionally. Such books have been written, but they obscure the real lessons of history found in the Bible. The biblical tree, we must always remember, bore the knowledge of both good *and* evil. The Bible—with all its horrors—reflects the societies in which its books were written. The societies of the biblical writers were *human* societies. Hostility, injustice, and war were then, and remain today, imponderable but real ingredients in any credible history.

The failure to understand the Bible's stories in their historic sense has unfortunately been used by some to give divine sanction to their own murderous actions and social injustices. Mark Twain gave an illustration of this tendency in his autobiography. He wrote:

> In my school days I had no aversion to slavery. I was not aware of anything wrong about it . . . . The local pulpit taught us that it was a holy thing, and that God

approved it. The doubter need only look in the Bible if he wanted to settle his mind—and then the texts were read aloud to make matters sure.[3]

Twain adds an illuminating social comment as he describes his mother's religious experience. She was a kindhearted and compassionate woman, but Twain remarks,

I think she was not conscious that slavery was a grotesque and unwarranted usurpation. She had never heard it assailed in any pulpit, but had heard it defended and sanctified in a thousand; her ears were familiar with Bible texts that approved it.[4]

The slavery issue is but one glaring example of the folly of accepting the words found in the Bible *without discrimination*. Anyone who reads the Bible in any thorough way will discover passages that seem to vindicate cruelty and brutality. These passages are reflections of an age that was often cruel and brutal, not necessarily reflections of a cruel and brutal God. For, along with these passages, there are others, passages which breathe a spirit of peace and forgiveness. There is, for example, the injunction to love your enemies and to do good to those who use you harshly.

We face frustration if we seek to find in a book, infallible though it might be in a universal sense, definite answers to our specific problems. Some of the Bible's writers faced life with an unfaltering faith and trust in a kind and benevolent God; others found life to be filled with vanity and vexation of spirit. Life is both—and neither.

The difficulties created by faith in a Bible seen as the infallible word of God can be overcome in great part by turning to history. The doctrine of the Bible's infallibility arose after the Protestant Reformation; until then, the only source of authority and faith was the Pope. The Church defined doctrines. People were actively discouraged from reading the Bible. There was a well-founded fear that if the common people read the Bible they would make their own private judgments. This, leaders thought, would destroy the unity of the Church and lead to heresies and divisions. Judging from the number of churches nowadays, this was clearly an accurate prediction.

After the Reformation, the power and authority of the Pope declined. The common people were caught in what might be called a belief gap. They were confused and distracted by being directed to the Bible as their new source of faith. Even if they had bibles, they did not necessarily know how to read! But Luther supported the change, saying that the Holy Spirit could only speak through the word of God—and that could only be found in the Scriptures. Luther further proclaimed that this word must be accepted literally. The Pope's fears became reality. Following the advent of the printing press, bibles became available to all. But in an illiterate society there were inevitable divisions and schisms, all of which led to riots, massacres, and full-scale religious wars.

The wars between Catholic princes and Protestant nobles ostensibly began for religious reasons, but they quickly turned into struggles for political control over respective provinces and states. Guelphs and Ghibellines in Italy, Tudors and Stuarts in England, Bourbons and Republicans in France—how much of their hatred came from religion and how much from the desire for power? There were also savage conflicts and persecutions encouraged by the different Protestant leaders. Calvin in Geneva had Servetus burned at the stake and even refused him a cleaner death by the sword because of a dispute over the words used in the sacrament of the Lord's Supper.

That all these holocausts were caused by differences in the interpretation of a holy book would sound incredible—if we had not witnessed a repetition of such savagery on an even larger scale in Ireland and the Middle East during the past fifty years.

A seemingly non-violent, but no less fanatical struggle is visible among zealous young people today. Some of these young people support their views with a strong faith in the infallibility of the Scriptures, as interpreted by the self-styled messiah from Korea, Sun Myung Moon. The Moonies, as they are known, are united by a fanatical drive for personal evangelism. Not to be outdone, other scripturists like the Charismatic Renewalists are pressing their messages on young people. Are they converting or are they brainwashing?

There are some obvious similarities between these new movements and the churches of my childhood. In the first part of this chapter I recalled the obsession of my neighborhood churches with the future life. Because of this otherworldly interest, there was little concern with the visible injustices in peoples' own backyards. The faithful would be rewarded in heaven, and the sinners would be punished in hell—so why worry over the swiftly-passing ills of this life? Thus earthly evils simmered, only to erupt in the bitterness of the past few decades.

There were a few people who were aware of these conditions. I well recall my own mother's questions. She was active in the church, but she seemed to see more clearly than most the contrasts between declarations of faith in personal salvation and an easy acceptance of the injustices apparent in the life around us. She had grown up immediately after the Civil War and had only about eight years of schooling. She admitted that she didn't know the answers or the remedies. Filled with despair, she would say, "I know it isn't right, but I don't know what to do about it." But when talking about the bitter denominational quarrels she would remark, "I don't know how we expect to get along together in heaven, when we do so poorly here on earth." Such an attitude was considered part of the heresy of works.

There is always room for disagreement about matters of faith. "God's house," says the Bible, "has many mansions." There are many interpretations of the mysterious universe that surrounds us. But our differences could be less bitter and more intelligently shared if we understood how the various portions of the Bible were written and how the Hebrew faith and the Christian religion arose out of the early history of the race.

Through his deep and prolonged work in translating the Bible, Dr. James Moffatt proposes three questions which could guide us in our search. Speaking of the people of the Bible, he asks:

1. Who were these people?
2. Where and how did they live?
3. What were the forms and functions of their literature?

Such are the questions which must be answered before we can read the Bible intelligently. Only when we understand what the Bible really is can we make valid judgments of its abiding worth for us all.

2

Creation Controversy

At the beginning of time there was water, only water in the starless night of the lifeless interval between dissolution and creation. All the potentialities of subsequent evolution rested, dormant and undifferentiated, in the primeval sea.

The Egyptians called it Nun, the ocean or shapeless magma containing all the seeds of life.

The earth may have floated in the midst of it like the yolk of an egg, if the Chinese were right. Or the magnificent lotus may have grown on it, and a Divine Being may have risen from the depths through the stem of the lotus, as the Indians have it. If this version is correct, He ordered some animals to bring him mud from the bottom of the sea, and with this He fashioned the earth.

Or perhaps Izanagi and Izanami came forward, together over the floating bridge of heaven—just over Japan—and plunged a jewel-bedecked celestial spear into the ocean of chaos that stretched beneath them. They stirred it until the liquid coagulated and thickened. When they withdrew the spear, drops of brine fell from it and formed the beginning of the world, an island "that coagulated of its own accord."

Elisabeth Mann Borgese
The Drama of the Oceans (New York: Abrams, 1976).

The very idea of creation is baffling. Despite scientific speculation, the creation of the earth remains a mystery. Creation escapes rational thinking; but the religious catechisms make it all sound simple. Catechisms state that God made the world. This simplistic answer was challenged by the little girl who, leaving church, asked her minister: "Who made God?" He couldn't answer, for, like all thinkers throughout history, he didn't know. The problem of first cause cannot be answered; it remains a mystery to both science and religion. Were things really created out of nothing, or have the elements from which the earth was created always existed? Either position confounds logical processes of thought. The endless succession of whys is perhaps the main impulse behind faith.

For all races, the search for origins is a primary drive. The answer of the ancestors of the Hebrews was recorded in the Book of Genesis (see particularly Genesis 1–10). These prehistoric persons were not scientists, but they had imagination. They contemplated the wonders of the earth and sky, and out of their meditations they created stories and myths to answer the question. Around these stories they devised ways of worshipping the unknown.

The familiar stories of Genesis are part of the folklore of the Western world. Everyone has heard of Adam and Eve, the first inhabitants of the planet. They were created fully grown and supposedly mature by a special act of creation. Placed in a garden of abundance, but tempted by a serpent, they ate forbidden fruit and were mercilessly driven from their fabled home. As the story continues, it becomes clear that not only Adam and Eve, but all their descendants down to the present, have been penalized because of their sin. Both "Where did we come from?" and "Why are we here?" get answered in this profound tale. The story of Adam and Eve has not been accepted as folklore by all readers of the Bible. A surprising number regard it as a factual account of creation. I cannot remember ever hearing it doubted when I was growing up. It was considered part of the revelation from God to man. Despite the proof of evolution, this position is held by a large minority of people today, the dubious legacy of a continuing controversy.

The fact that this controversy continues may be seen in the recent dismissal of several prominent professors from their positions in one of the largest Protestant seminaries in this country. The reason? The professors doubted the factual nature of the creation stories—they preferred to term them myths. Perhaps these dissenters should consider themselves lucky—heresy was, until recently, a heinous crime punished by imprisonment, torture, or death.

But the heat of theological battle is not restricted to ivory towers—in recent years some school board members have been forced to answer charges of heretical malfeasance in office. After one demonstration, zealous parents demanded that the Genesis story be accorded equal importance with the scientific study of cosmic creation and evolution.

This account of creation told in the first chapter of Genesis states that "in the beginning, God created," and then goes on to narrate how God created the sun, the moon, and the stars, and the planet earth with its vegetation and animal life as well as the first man and woman. It was, according to the account, all done in six days. On the seventh God rested, pronouncing that all he had done was good. As the story continues, we read that he had doubts about the wisdom of his efforts. Human society, though created by God, proceeded by its own fallible ways into one form of corruption after another. Finally, God decided to wipe it all out with a flood, destroying everything except Noah, his family, and two of every species of living creatures on the earth. We're advised that if the lesson doesn't work it'll be "the fire next time."

The explanation of creation given in Genesis is, we must remember, the product of human efforts to understand superhuman events. As such, it must stand along side all other efforts of man's imagination. One of the most compelling of these, because it is more consistent with physical evidence, is Darwin's theory of evolution. Simply stated, Darwin's theory proposes that the earth and man evolved over a long slow process of creation—a creation involving millions of years. It may be thought of as a myth—but it is a *logical* myth and therefore more attuned to our sophisticated scientific age.

Zealots, both biblical and scientific, may argue their points of view for years to come, but as an inquisitive student I am more interested in the derivation of the creation stories in Genesis. We accept Darwin's theory because we know who created it, on what basis, and with what tools. But what do we know about the Genesis stories? How did they originate? Who wrote them? When were they written?

Since Genesis is the opening book of the Bible, it is natural to infer that it was the first written and oldest book of the collection. But the general consensus of present day scholars is that Genesis and the other four books of the Pentateuch were among the latest of the Old Testament books to be completed. They were produced later than the historic books, even later than the writings of the eighth century B.C. prophets. Dr. Edgar J. Goodspeed, an eminent Bible scholar, dates the editing of the Pentateuch around the year 350 B.C.

Though not completed until this late period in Hebrew history, these books contain all the traditions from which the nation evolved. They were compiled out of ancient legends and handed down by word of mouth for perhaps a thousand years before people began to write them down.

Preserved in the memory of successive generations over centuries, these stories were gathered up by writers in the eighth and seventh centuries B.C. into a number of documents (known to scholars as the J.D.E.P. documents). These documents were doubtless used by the final compilers of these books four centuries later.

The authorship of these stories about the early times (known as the Pentateuch) is therefore unknown, but there has been a lingering belief that Moses was responsible. According to Professor Samuel Sandmel of the Hebrew Union College, Moses' status as the originator of the creation myth was not doubted by the Jewish community until the twelfth century of the present era; indeed, some groups still believe it today. However, according to Professor Sandmel, this theory is no longer held by scholars; they recognize that no one man could have created so complex and profound a tale. It is precisely this superhuman power which leads some to call the work God's.

A more important question arises. Why were these books, dealing with prehistoric times, produced at such a late date in Hebrew history? The answer is that these books were published during a time of crisis in the life of the Hebrew people—a crisis following a period of great trouble and uncertainty, a time when it was doubtful if the nation could be re-established. The Hebrew people needed this revival of their ancient heritage in order to strengthen their faith in themselves as a special race—a people called by Yahweh to a great destiny.

This crisis came about as the result of the destruction of the city of Jerusalem and the demolition of its magnificent temple by the Babylonians in 586 B.C. Following the destruction of their city, the Jewish people were scattered, and their leaders were exiled to Babylon. After fifty years the leaders returned from exile. They found Israel in a state of chaos. The people, their will and confidence shattered by conquest, had deserted their faith in Yahweh. They had turned to other gods. Moreover, they had violated the strongest decree of Yahweh by intermarrying with people who worshipped foreign gods (see Ezra and Nehemiah).

To correct these lapses and to restore the faith, the Hebrew leaders called for a revival of the ancient traditions and for a restatement of their long history. Accordingly, the priests and the scribes began to collect the records of the distant past from the ruins of their temple and archives, and to amend their ancient laws—which had previously been codified as "the laws of Moses." This body of material has been known since as "the Law," or the sacred Torah, of the religion of Judaism.

The universal desire of nations to restate their traditions of the past periodically can be appreciated by observing similar movements in the United States today. The many bicentennial celebrations in 1976 were attempts to dramatize the traditions of early American history, and thereby to elicit renewed respect and greater loyalty to them.

But when any nation attempts to recover its past, it discovers that the facts have been overlaid with fiction, legends and myths. No matter how erroneous these ancient legends are, or how much they misstate a nation's virtues, they are still the most important part of a nation's heritage. In them is preserved the people's faith in their institutions and the religion they profess. By retaining and amplifying certain key events—such as the Revolutionary Army's winter at Valley Forge, which most patriots turned away from as a tragic misery, but which later generations celebrated as a triumphant testing—a people creates its own history. Arnold Toynbee suggests that this transformation of stories into legends is the way all histories are written:

> History, like the drama and the novel, grew out of mythology. A primitive form of apprehension and expression in which—as in fairy tales listened to by children or in dreams dreamt by adults—the line between fact and fiction is left undrawn. It has been said of the Iliad that anyone who starts reading it as history will find it full of fiction, but, equally, anyone who starts reading it as fiction will find it full of history.[5]

Toynbee's suggestion is supported by the histories written of any nation. Roman history, for example, begins with the legend of Romulus and Remus, two babies suckled by a wolf. These two babies eventually became the founders of the city of Rome. Similarly, Greek history begins with the myths of the gods and goddesses of Hellas and the early legends of the Trojan wars. And American history has preserved the legends of our early settlers. One has only to look at the Bunyanesque folklore that has developed around the lives of Washington, Lincoln, Daniel Boone and Davy Crockett to see this phenomenon at work. Each new anecdote confirms a different ideal, teaches another part of the social lesson.

Because the stories brought together by the compilers of the Pentateuch were prehistoric, they are more imaginative than factual. Without any scientific knowledge to rely on, these early guessers substituted their gift of imagination. We cannot afford to forget that they were primitive people, who looked out upon the world of nature and were impressed, daunted, hopeful. They were awed by a roll of thunder or a deadly flash of lightning. While dreaming their dreams and fashioning their myths, they filled the world with unseen spirits that had the power to control the movements of the heavens and the forces of the earth.

As described by the writers of Genesis, these early citizens of the earth regarded the heavens as a solid dome above which lived the gods. From time to time the gods visited the earth. Commerce between the two spheres was vividly imaged in Jacob's dream of a ladder which reached from heaven to earth. Down it came angels to minister to him; up it he was carried when his life was done. In their fear and wonder, these early inhabitants built rude altars (at first only piles of rough stones) to placate the powers dwelling in the heavens and tempt them to take up residence on earth. Elaborate sacrifices were burned on the altars because the worshippers felt that the gods were pleased with the savory odors. In Genesis 11 it is recorded that earthbound humans tried to erect a tower into heaven. They wished to discover its secrets and thus make a name for themselves. They were thwarted in their efforts (a recognition of practical limitations), their tower was destroyed (a lesson in how pride is punished) and they were reduced to babble (an attempt to explain the existence of many languages in a small area). The story of Babel is a model of how and why the myths of the Bible came to be.

These stories and legends must accordingly be considered within the different time spans in which they originated. Dr. James Moffatt stresses the part which imagination played in the early stories. Moffatt states:

> For the premonarchial period—the period before Saul and David—and especially for the period prior to the Egyptian Exodus—it was needful to use imagination more than memory, though all memory is more or less imaginative. No one had written down the stories of the patriarchs during their lifetime, or even after it. Memory operated in the transmission of such tales, but more in the shaping of the traditions which followed.[6]

Dr. Moffatt's explanation would be understood by any child who has played "telephone" or "gossip" (the game that has a phrase or story whispered around a circle). Moffatt recognizes that stories grow as they are transmitted from one person to another. Thus the skilled narrators who kept Old Testament stories alive over the centuries magnified and perhaps transformed them. They retained the pointedly fantastic stories of Adam and Eve, and gloried in the prowess of their ancestral heroes because that was what held the audiences through the moral lessons. Age was honored, so the patriarchs were given exceptionally long lives. Methuselah, at 969 years, is the champion of this tendency. Giants, perhaps people of another race taller than the five-foot average of the Hebrews, were explained as the offspring of the "sons of God" and the "daughters of men."

These highly imaginative stories found in the first books of the Bible were gathered in permanent form in around 721 B.C. from two previously written documents. These documents were the J document, representing the viewpoint of the southern tribes, and the E document, representing the viewpoint of the northern tribes. In 721 B.C. they were brought together and scholars now speak of them as the JE source. These early stories were collected much as Pete Seeger and Alan Lomax gathered the stories and ballads of the isolated regions of Appalachia in the forties and fifties. The Hebrew writers, however, altered and embellished their stories to fit the tribal loyalty and doctrinal sophistication of the different writers.

Though these first documents telling the Hebrews' pre-history are long ago fallen into dust, research scholars of the past two centuries are convinced that they did exist. Through differences in language, structure, occasional duplications, and the use of different words to indicate the deity, scholars have detected a great deal of evidence indicating several sources used in compiling the first books. In the final compilation, the combined JE document was used in conjunction with the Priestly or P document. One can see how this was done by reading from Dr. Moffatt's translation of Genesis. In this translation the JE document is printed in one type style, the P document in another. These different documents have been fitted together much as a school boy might write an essay, taking a paragraph from one book and following that with a paragraph from another book or magazine.

One can also follow the development of the scholars' theory of multiple sources by observing in any translation the two stories of creation in Genesis, each giving a different sequence and using a different style of writing. The first story starts in the first chapter and extends to the fourth verse of the second chapter—this comes from the P source. The other story, from the JE source, follows.

The J document is certainly the most vivid of the writings. The writer is revealed, even in translation, as a master storyteller. In his writings we find the dramatic stories of man's beginnings, the stories of Adam and Eve, Cain and Abel, Abraham and Isaac, and those of Jacob and his twelve sons. Many of the stories of these early times reveal primitive touches. God is portrayed as a kind of folk hero. One such story depicts God walking just like a man in the garden in the cool of the day calling out to Adam who runs and hides himself. Some of these and other stories of the type have been delightfully retold in Roarck Bradford's *Ol' Man Adam an' His Chillun* (Harper and Bros; 1928). Bradford even takes it a bit further in his imagination and has God attend a fish fry with his people, blowing up much "firmament" for them to drink.

An important element to be noted in the stories from the J account is that the characters are portrayed in their vices as well as their virtues. The writers were not consciously trying to write Sacred Scripture. They were merely "passing it on," and though in the process they glorified their ancient forebears, they couldn't help but "tell it like it was." (For more on this process, see the Appendix.)

Because of the nature of J's writings, the earthiness, the portrayal of the folk nature of God, as well as the portrayal of the vices of the fathers of the race, some biblical scholars today feel that the Priestly writers of the fourth century B.C. felt compelled to write their own story of creation. These writers had a heightened moral insight gained through the thousand years of Hebrew history since the gathering of the J stories. Their religious thinking had been influenced by the writings of the eighth century B.C. prophets (see Chapter 5 of this book). They used the Babylonian myth of creation as a model (but elevated both the moral tone and the literary style of this ancient story), as well as the story of creation told by the J writers as found in the second chapter of Genesis. God was no longer presented as a folk hero of the Hebrew people, but as the exalted ruler of the universe— the one God over all.

The Priestly writers of the fourth century B.C. are credited with gathering the material from many sources in compiling the sacred books of the Hebrews—the first five books of the Bible. In doing so, they did not discard the more earthy stories from the J sources. Nor did they delete the faults of the patriarchs as told in them. These were too much a part of the heritage of the race. But in their writings the Priestly writers wove around the accounts in J a sense of God's concern for the ancient forebears, and of his faith in them as the future leaders in the developing nation.

There is another aspect of these early stories which has had a profound effect upon the theology of the Christian Church. For the stories of creation also reveal a much later, sophisticated development. There are mythic qualities in many of these early stories. The story of Eve carrying on a profound philosophical discussion with a serpent about the nature of good and evil is certainly mythological. Likewise, the story of the forbidden fruit has the character of a myth. The fruit, popularly referred to as an apple, is far more sophisticated than that. It is a metaphoric fruit, the symbol of "the knowledge of good and evil." Though no one knows exactly what the writer meant by this abstract concept, we all can feel the power of his symbol—we see our own acts "bear fruit" for good or ill each day.

Orthodox theologians have used the stories of Adam and Eve to explain the sinfulness of all mankind. They have called Adam's sin the Original Sin—a sin that taints all persons. But such explanations can go too far, as they did when medieval theologians condemned women by making them bear an inferior status, or claimed they suffered the pains of childbirth as a direct result of Eve's sin.

Such interpretations aside, the stories of Genesis show a high degree of literary skill. They have furnished one of the main sources of folklore in the West and they remain the source of much of the poetry, music, and art of our civilization. But more, they illustrate better than any other body of myth the tendency for all races and cultures to express their religious ideology in simple yet complex stories, legends, and myths. This tendency was pointed out by Harvey Cox in the opening pages of his book *The Seduction of the Spirit*. Speaking of religion as "a story and signal," he wrote:

> All human beings have an innate need to tell and hear stories, and to have a story to live by. Religion, whatever else it has done, has provided one of the main ways of meeting this abiding need. Most religions begin as a cluster of stories, embedded in saga, rite, and rehearsal . . .the Hebrew Scriptures are largely stories, so is the New Testament. Rabbis, saints, Zen masters, and gurus of every persuasion convey their holy teachings by jokes, parables, allegories, anecdotes, and fables. There has never been a better raconteur than Jesus of Nazareth himself.[7]

But that gets us ahead of our story; the sophisticated narrative of the New Testament is a product of the long apprenticeship in mythic narration served by the writers of Genesis and the other vitally important books of the Old Testament.

3

Ancestors

Those who search old records to trace their genealogy often wind up "choosing" their ancestors. That is, they find a few persons in their ancestral records whom they delight in remembering and whose achievements they proudly relate, and they claim them; the others are ignored.

After all, you cannot honor all your ancestors—you don't know them all. If you go back only ten generations in your search (as you do if you're a member of the D.A.R.) there are more than a thousand! Out of that vast number almost any of you can find a few forebears who will lend historical significance to your life. This historical identity, this sense of roots in time and place, is important, as borne out by the fact that almost every family has someone who makes the search.

Once, while in London, I succumbed to the desire to know my roots. I spent some time looking up family records, and I was moderately successful. That is, I found one man with my name. What's most significant about my search is that I stopped looking after finding this one man—he was a heretic who was drawn and quartered! My wife has had even better success in this line. She points with pride to an ancestor whose picture hangs in the Essex Institute in Salem, Massachusetts—he was put to death as a witch. We have both decided it's more relevant to honor our own fathers and mothers. To delve deeper into our lineage is, as we found, a risky business; who knows *what* we'd find.

Individuals are not always able to identify persons of distinction in their heritage, but nations certainly can. Each country and each race cannily fosters stories of its legendary characters who sought to preserve the qualities of heroism and high devotion in their day. Consider how England treasures the memory of Alfred the Great, who really lived, and King Arthur and his band of noble knights, who didn't.

This same experience was true of the Hebrew tribes. They looked through their store of prehistoric traditions and found two men who stood out: Abraham and Moses. These two ghosts of the past, out of thousands remembered by one group or another, gave historical signficance and a sense of heroic destiny to the seekers. Abraham's significance resides in his gift of God's promise. In Genesis 12 it is recorded that God said to him:

> Leave your country, leave your kindred, leave your father's house, for a land that I will show to you; I will make a great nation of you, and make you famous for your bliss; those who bless you, I will bless, and anyone who curses you, I will curse, till all the nations of the earth seek bliss such as yours (Moffatt's translation).

A variation of this same promise exists in Genesis 17, taken from another of the documents making up that book. It seems to be a later account, most probably one made after Israel's establishment. Here Abraham's God speaks of the compact which He made with Abraham.

> I will give to you and your descendants the land where you are residing, the whole of the land of Canaan, as a possession for all times, and I will be their God (Moffatt's translation).

Moses, the other symbolic ancestor, came later. He led the tribes of the Hebrews out of slavery in Egypt, established the religion of Yahweh, and became known as the "Great Emancipator and Lawgiver of the Hebrews."

Through all the centuries of their existence, the Hebrew people were admonished to remember these two honored forebears, for they furnished the traditions upon which the tenets of both the Hebrew and the Christian religions are based. Through the legends of Abraham and Moses, the Hebrews learned that God (Yahweh) had chosen them, and that He had led them from slavery, through trial and tribulation, to their Promised Land.

However, these stories and legends raised questions about the nature of Abraham's visions and Moses' conversations with God. It is impossible to say what basis in fact exists in these ancient legends. It becomes a matter of faith, or even credulity, to accept as fact stories of God's actually speaking to people. Certain obvious questions must be raised: How much are we directed by supernatural power? How much are the objects of our faith created in our minds by our own desires? How much does our faith give support to our hopes and wishes? Are there other explanations for the miracles of the Bible?

A recent hypothesis proposed by Dr. Hans Goedicke of Johns Hopkins University suggests that there may be a naturalistic explanation for at least one of the biblical stories. Dr. Goedicke, as reported in the *New York Times* (May 11, 1981), claims to have evidence that indicates that the miracle of the "parting of the waves" did in fact take place, as the result of an earthquake in 1477 B.C. Such a claim need not disturb the faithful; after all, God could as easily start an earthquake as part the waters more directly.

Whether the incidents recorded in Genesis are factual or not, they indicate much concerning a people's hopes and beliefs. Before we discuss Moses further, we must first consider the story of Abraham as found in Genesis 11–15. In it, Abraham is portrayed as a wealthy man. He has great herds of cattle and always needs more grazing lands, but he is magnanimous. He is also faithful to his God; his great test comes when he is willing to prove his devotion to God by sacrificing his only son on the altar. This story is now seen by authorities as an attempt to halt the custom of child sacrifice, which had persisted over the centuries, even up until the time of the writing of this legend. In the Genesis story, Abraham hears the voice of God refusing his sacrifice and directing him to leave his ancestral lands and move into lands inhabited by other nations and races. Abraham's descendants will possess that new land forever, God promises. God further promises that He will go with them, and that they will be His Chosen People. This last promise represents one of the great breakthroughs of faith, from an animistic belief in resident spirits to a theological faith in an ever-present diety. Nevertheless, the question remains: Where does the legend of a faithful man leave off, and the acquisitive desire of a sly herdsman begin?

A persistent question arises in the mind of the skeptical person: Where does Abraham's God come from? This is a natural question when one recalls that in the time of Abraham, and certainly in the stories told in these early books, there was no thought of a universal God ruling over all of life. It was a time of many gods. There were nature gods, household gods and personal deities. Sometimes these gods were worshipped in family shrines, sometimes in images shaped like humans called seraphim (see the story of Laban in Genesis 30). It seems, from this legend, that one of these local gods spoke to Abraham and adopted him. Instead of being embodied in the form of some natural object (a bush, for example), Abraham's God allowed Himself to be personified. From this adoption and transformation, the Hebrews developed their concept of God, known as Yahweh, and pledged their faith for His promise to them.

There is an imaginary interpretation of this legend, found in a whimsical autobiography of Yahweh entitled *I Yahweh*, written by Robert Munson Grey. In this book Grey describes how an ancestral family deity, jealous of the honors being paid to the great tribal gods through the pageantry of temple worship, attached himself to Abraham. He lured Abraham to his service by offering to make him the founder of a great nation. Grey points out that as Abraham grew in power and prestige, so did Yahweh grow in stature. Yahweh's power and glory continued to expand under the leadership of the great kings, David and Solomon, until He became the only comprehensive symbol of the nation's power. To his worshippers he became the Lord of Hosts, the leader of the Hebrew armies against their enemies. When the followers of Yahweh were loyal to their faith, his priests claimed Yahweh made them victorious; when they lost, the priests found some sin which had caused Yahweh to remove his protection. Yahweh was a brave god; he would literally lead his Chosen People into battle, inside a small wooden shrine called the Ark of the Covenant which was carried in front of the battle line. On one occasion, the Ark was captured by the Philistines, and the Hebrew army was a shambles until the Ark was recaptured.

The legends of these two patriarchs, Abraham and Moses, as recorded in the books of Genesis and Exodus, have kept alive the faith of the Hebrew people in themselves. For four thousand years they have seen themselves as a unique race and they traditionally regard themselves as God's Chosen People. Different segments of the Hebrew people, however, have offered divergent interpretations of this claim.

A few Jews reject the Chosen People concept outright. The term "Chosen People," according to one Jewish writer, has been weighed down with too many uncomfortable implications, such as undue pride and a frequent "martyr complex." But many other Jews proudly regard the designation as laying a holy obligation upon the Jewish people. This large majority claims to have been charged with the responsibility of transmitting the laws and prophetic insights of their heritage to all people. A representative of this viewpoint, Dr. Mordecai Kaplan, sees all people as potentially called by God. He says, "In a sense, every great people that has contributed to enlightenment and progress is chosen of God."

Nevertheless, the implications of this tradition that the Jews are the Chosen People, embedded as it is in Sacred Scripture, have created more misunderstanding and persecution than admiration. So much has this been true that one can sympathize with Tevye, the patriarch in "Fiddler on the Roof," when he says, "Lord, we know we are your Chosen People; but once in a while, couldn't you choose someone else?"

Perhaps the heaviest responsibility Jews entail from being "chosen" lies in the demand that they be champions for those not so blessed—a situation which in our own day has meant that Jews are found in the forefront of every fight for social equality. The burden is even heavier because of the example set by the other prehistoric ancestor of the Hebrew people, Moses. The Book of Exodus is entirely Moses' story, and as deliverer/prophet/lawgiver he has made a greater impact upon the Hebrews than anyone else in their religious memory.

Though there is little historic verification for Moses' story from any source outside the Bible, Moses emerges from the pages of the Bible as the most commanding figure of the Hebrew legends. His story has made a lasting stamp on the national consciousness of the Jews. As one writer put it, "No figure out of legend, no creation of mythology could have been so real for so long a time without a historical base." A contemporary scholar, Dr. James Fleming, states in his study of historical characters in the Old Testament that without Moses "there would, humanly speaking, be no Old Testament, no Jewish people, no Judaism, and no Christian Church; perhaps also no religion of Islam." If Abraham is responsible for the Jews' belief in their God, Moses is responsible for the shape of that belief and the very shape of their lives.

The account of Moses in Exodus follows the well-known narrative of Joseph, as found in the last chapters of Genesis. Joseph, the favorite son of Jacob, was sold into slavery by his jealous brothers. He was taken to Egypt where, though a slave, he attained distinction (with God's help) in the court of Pharaoh, and was entrusted with great responsibilities. Joseph was discovered in Egypt by the same brothers who had sent him into near certain death years before. They had come to buy grain in a time of famine in their own land. Not only did he forgive them and give them food, but he urged them to settle in Egypt under his protection. As many parents throughout history have done, Jacob moved to be near his successful son. Moreover, many other Hebrews followed Jacob, until finally there was a large Hebrew colony settled in the land of Egypt.

As the years went by, the alien Hebrews became slaves in the land of their adoption. As the story is told, Pharaoh became frightened by the great increase in numbers of these alien people in his land. In his fear he enslaved them and sought to limit their numbers. It is a story familiar to all those who remember the Nazi warnings that the brown-skinned races were breeding faster than the white, and would therefore soon take over by sheer weight of numbers. Not only did the Pharaoh "lay murderous burdens upon the Hebrews," but he resorted to a notoriously harsh and brutal measure: he ordered that all male Hebrew babies be put to death. It was during these times of repression that Moses was born.

Even those with only a slight acquaintance with Bible legends know the story of how Moses' mother saved her newborn son. She set him in a basket among the bulrushes of the river Nile. There he was discovered by the daughter of Pharaoh. She brought him to the palace, adopted him, and raised him as a prince. Though he was considered a noble ornament to the household of Pharaoh, young Moses turned his back upon the luxury of the palace; he became instead the leader of the slaves in their spectacular escape from Egypt.

The story of Moses' Exodus is filled with miraculous incidents and exciting accounts of his confrontations with the Pharaoh and with God, or Yahweh. These accounts, with their triumphal end, have kept hope alive among the Jewish people through centuries of repeated persecutions. Around this story the Jewish people have woven their most joyous ritual, the celebration of Passover.

This divine escape from slavery also gave hope to two centuries of black slaves in America. These pitiful people voiced their hopes in songs about Moses, singing, "Go down Moses, and let my people go." Slaves before the Civil War sang, "Steal away, steal away to Jesus" to signal the departure of a contingent of slaves on the freedom bound underground railway; but they sang to Moses when they sought a universal deliverance.

The escape of Moses and the Hebrews, and their subsequent wandering in the wilderness, as they attempted to reach the Promised Land, marks the real beginning of Hebrew history. It was only at this time that they began to keep written records in the new alphabet that was probably the Jews' greatest inheritance of their Egyptian enslavement. However, much of this history remains clouded with uncertainty. Too many legendary incidents are accepted as fact by doctrinaire believers; they are not accorded this credence by present-day scholars. For instance, scholars do not accept as fact the great invasion of the lands of the Canaanites, with its set battles, dramatized by biblical writers. Scholarly inquiry indicates that there was, on the contrary, a slow infiltration of these lands by separate tribes. It was a process which went on for generations, even centuries. Minor skirmishes took place (at Jericho, for example) as various tribes settled on land claimed by other people, but it took five hundred years before David unified the tribes and established the Hebrew kingdom.

Another disputed incident is the biblical account of the reception of the law. After the escape from Egypt, it is written that Moses went up on the mountain, where he received the law from Yahweh. Almost everyone is familiar with this account, which is found in both Exodus and Deuteronomy. Moses descended from the mountain bringing the Ten Commandments, written on tablets of stone. This scene, as over-dramatized in the movie produced by Cecil B. DeMille, is perhaps the best-known—and least valid—picture the general public has of biblical history.

For Moses brought not only the Ten Commandments, but also the whole body of laws by which the Hebrew people were to be governed. This voluminous material forms the second part of Exodus, and all of Deuteronomy and Leviticus. Carved in stone, these laws would have required the whole forty years the Hebrews wandered in the wilderness to write and explain, never mind to carry. Scholars therefore doubt this account of Moses formulating this vast body of laws. They interpret these laws as representing in part an earlier formulation of rules for the Hebrew tribes during their nomadic existence. Moses' achievement lies probably in refining them to serve as laws applicable to a more settled society. They clearly represent insights which were obtained after the people traded their nomadic existence for the more settled life in Canaan. Some laws, for example, deal with the preservation of landmarks and the settlement of debts—both of value only to a sedentary people. There are also rules for the treatment of slaves by their owners. At the same time there are sections which were clearly not revised to fit changing circumstances. Often, for example, the laws speak of evicted people taking their tents with them—but by this time the Hebrews were almost all living in stone and clay buildings, not tents.

This presence of both primitive and contemporary laws in one volume leads to frequent contradictions. There is a wide divergence of ethical standards represented in these laws, some based on the harsh early life and others stemming from the time of civilization, which creates problems for critical readers of the Bible. Many are troubled by the seemingly vicious demands made by Yahweh at times. There are, for example, laws which call for absurdly stern penalties for minor infractions. According to the law, heretics and rebellious sons must be stoned to death. In addition, severe restraints are arbitrarily put on innocent persons. One law, for instance, prohibits bastards or their descendants for ten generations from entering the congregation. Of course, such laws were most likely created as deterrents; in the second case, for example, it was expected that fathers would legitimize their children, and the law merely added encouragement.

On the other hand, many of the mosaic laws reflect a growing humane concern. These latter laws show the liberal influence of the eighth century B.C. prophets. Some of these more humane provisions protected slaves from callous slave holders, and others protected the runaway slave. One very important law established cities of refuge, where individuals could escape mob justice and wait for a calmer time when justice could be done. Some laws protected widows and orphans; other codifications reached into the business world, with provisions for the protection of debtors. For instance, a debt was to be forgiven after seven years, and loans to fellow Israelites were to be made without interest.

We who look back critically upon the different levels of ethical insight in these codifications must consider two contributing historical factors: First, the laws were formulated over the course of centuries; second, books of codifications in all cultures are seldom weeded out. We in America remember how difficult it was in the sixties to revise laws that denied civil rights to blacks and Indians. *Reader's Digest* has for years been able to fill empty pages with samples of eighteenth and nineteenth century laws that have never been taken off the books. The ancient hostilities of the Hebrews, and the more rugged conditions of their earlier times, remain mirrored in their law books despite the priest's repeated efforts to revise them.

From the beginning, the Jewish people have been influenced by the traditions of Abraham and Moses. During this critical time, the basic tenets of their faith were organized. Both the traditions and the laws have been clarified since then by generations of scribes, teachers and prophets, to the point where the full Jewish law runs to literally millions of words. It is probable that no nation in history has ever tried to put into religious laws such minute and complete regulation of daily life; Orthodox Jewish people still practice many of the regulations set down in the law books of the Pentateuch. The longevity of the faith must be due in large measure to this continuity. Arnold Toynbee, struck by the capacity of the Jewish people to survive through terrible times, called their ability to keep their original culture intact, and their spiritual integrity uncompromised, a story unique in history.

The house of Judah has not been without conflict, both from within and from without. But these conflicts have served to solidify rather than divide the faith, and from them has arisen a tapestry of Jewish culture which is enriched by time and struggle. Jews are imbued with a historical awareness of their religious heritage and responsibilities. This awareness is based on, and constantly tested by, the memory of the Jews' prehistoric ancestors—Abraham and Moses.

4

Show No Mercy

In the preceding chapter we discussed the different levels of ethical demands found in the ancient law books of the Hebrews. The portrayals of the God Yahweh in these books are equally complex. At times Yahweh is portrayed as kind and forgiving, a Heavenly Father alert to the needs of his children. At other times he is seen as a fierce War God, demanding that his people show no mercy toward defeated foes.

Not only was Yahweh a War God, he was also a jealous and unreasoning God who punished those who disobeyed his orders. Listen, for instance, to the words recorded in Exodus 20:

> For I, the Lord your God am a jealous God, punishing the children for the sins of the fathers, punishing them that hate me, down to the third and fourth generation, but showing kindness to thousands who love me and keep my commandments.

Later, in Exodus 32, Yahweh is so angry with his people that He says to Moses, "Let me alone, that my wrath may blaze against them and burn them up." As the story tells it, only the pleas of Moses deterred him.

As the great God above all gods, Yahweh was a segregationist. He demanded that his people live apart from the people of other nations and other religions. When they conquered other lands and moved onto them, Yahweh decreed that there was to be no intermarriage. They were, in fact, commanded to destroy the conquered people in order to remove any temptation. Listen to the instructions given to the Hebrews in the seventh chapter of Deuteronomy:

> When the Lord your God brings you into the land you are entering to take possession of it, and clears away all nations before you—nations greater and stronger than yourselves—and when the Lord gives them over to you, and you defeat them, you must utterly destroy them, and show no mercy unto them. You shall not make any marriages with them, taking their daughters for your sons, and giving your daughters to their sons, for they would turn your sons from following me, to serve other gods; then the anger of your Lord would be kindled against you, and he would destroy you quickly. Break down their altars, and burn their graven images with fire.

In order to evaluate this passage from Deuteronomy fairly, one must see it in the light of history, keeping in mind that the passage was written centuries after the events to which it refers. The words calling for the complete extermination of their enemies were put into the mouth of Moses by the writers of Deuteronomy. They were the injunctions which later writers thought should have been given to those preparing to invade the Promised Land. The order was, to these later writers, what they thought Yahweh really wanted, and what they wished had happened. But these things did *not* happen, certainly not as thoroughly as the writers of Deuteronomy wished. For the history of Israel's creation is filled with the exact opposite of this "God-given" dictum.

The records of the invasions with their many battles and conquered cities (as we have them in the books of Joshua, Judges, Samuel, and Kings) are highly romantic versions of history. These books were written at a much later time mainly to glorify the victories of the Jews' ancestors. In this glorification the writers certainly did not minimize the destruction of cities and the murder of their inhabitants, but they almost never record the total and complete destruction ordered by Yahweh in the Book of Deuteronomy. In fact, they report that the invaders settled peacefully among the defeated inhabitants and did intermarry with them. Moreover, the conquerers worshipped the gods of the conquered enemies. It was this ungodly behavior that incurred the wrath of later biblical writers. We know this process as "acculturation," the inevitable tendency of new arrivals in any society to adapt to existing customs and eventually lose their own cultural identity. The problem must have been especially marked with the Hebrews, who never formed a majority in any area they conquered.

It is no surprise, therefore, to read in Judges 3 the charges that were leveled against the Hebrews' behavior:

> As the Israelites lived among the Canaanites (and others) they married their daughters, married their own sons to their daughters, and sacrificed to their gods—forgetting their own God—and worshipped the baals and sacred poles.

The account in Judges goes on to say that the anger of the Eternal flamed hot against Israel, and He sold them into the power of their enemies.

The writers of Deuteronomy (writing around 621 B.C.) used hindsight to condemn their progenitors. Writing at a time of chaos during Josiah's reign (centuries after the reputed time of Moses), they proclaimed that all their troubles had come upon them because of the sins of their fathers. They had not obeyed Yahweh, they had not destroyed their enemies, they had intermarried with the people of false religions, and they had thereby weakened the uniqueness and purity of Hebrew life and religion.

Later, in the fourth century B.C., following the return from exile, the Priestly writers included Deuteronomy laws and ordinances in the newly revised laws (Pentateuch). In order to restore the life of Israel, root out false religions and re-establish the religion of Judaism, the religious leaders felt the need to underscore the concept of Yahweh as a fierce and unyielding God (see 2 Kings 22–23). To purify the religious life from its heresies, the leaders demanded that all people who had married foreign wives divorce them and send them back to the lands they came from. This effort was highlighted in the Book of Ezra. One can find an analogy to these efforts to purge Jerusalem of foreign elements in the religious revival of Jonathan Edwards in eighteenth century America. Edwards sought to frighten the unfaithful by reviving the threat of a stern Calvinist God. He drove people into hysterics with his vivid portrayal of sinners in "the hands of an angry God;" but he also helped solidify their faith and integrity while other colonies quickly lost all sense of a special mission.

This strict and aggressive policy by the religious leaders of Judea, in the time of crisis that followed their return from exile, had two long-term consequences. First, it grafted upon Judaism a strong opposition to intermarriage, and, second, it transformed Yahweh into a cruel God of War. The effect of the latter change has been to put biblical authority into the hands of militarists. One has but to glance through the pages of any history book to witness an unending parade of generals and war leaders prayerfully seeking guidance from the God "who is on our side." Recent history reveals troops in Vietnam receiving the blessing of chaplains before going out to burn villages. One soldier, who was confused over such sanctified killing, said, "Whatever we were doing...murder...atrocities...God was *always* on our side."

The fierce opposition to intermarriage created by the compilers of the Pentateuch was intensified by changes which occurred in Hebrew life as a result of settling in the land of the Canaanites. The process of acculturation was an age-old struggle between the long-established culture and religion of a settled agricultural people and the already-changing mores of a newcoming tribal and nomadic people. There resulted not only great changes in social, economic, and religious life of the Hebrew invaders, but also in the very nature of the God Yahweh. Under the circumstances, such changes were bound to occur.

Before moving onto the lands of the Canaanites, the Hebrews had enjoyed an austere but stable desert existence. Now they confronted a new and quite different culture, and the culture shock could not help but alter their own laws and mores. Prior to their move, the Hebrew tribes had been held together by strict rules governing health and morals, and they faithfully observed the bans on intermingling with other groups. They knew from tragic experience that without such unity life in the desert was impossible. Now, as they moved into a more settled community where their life was not so hard, they changed. There seemed to be more abundance, and with abundance comes a margin for error. People could—and did—experiment with sloth, greed and a general loosening of moral fibre, and they found that they could survive anyway.

The Canaanites, for example, worshipped fertility gods. Their rituals of worship often involved the use of temple prostitutes, and many of the Hebrews were tempted. What the Hebrews contended with is not unique. It is a problem confronting any nation when its puritanical standards break down before the temptations of more wealth and leisure. This is particularly true in times of war, when two cultures meet and irrevocably change one another. A famous song accented American fear of such exotic influence during the First World War: "How are you gonna keep 'em down on the farm after they've seen Paree?"

Another change occurred among the Hebrews when they moved from the tribal life of the desert into the more settled agricultural communities. They lost all sense of the close participation and common sharing which tribal desert organization demanded. In the desert it was either "one for all," or a quick death. The strong did not hoard while the weaker starved; they would be ruthlessly cut off if they tried. The land was for tribal use; it was not private property. There was, among the Hebrew tribes, a "*mishpat* justice"— a kind of survival relationship described by Graham Wallis: "The sources of life, land and water, are communal, not rightly disposed of by private persons through sale or exchange." It is out of tradition that Jews are generally liberal in matters of social justice, not out of simple self-protection.

By contrast, in the settled agricultural communities where the Hebrews moved, individualism prevailed and individual ownership of the land was the accepted custom. In the commercial civilization of Canaan, each man had to look out for himself. The weak were neglected or exploited, fostering class divisions visible in such scenes as King David's dancing before the Ark, to his wife's bitter disapproval. The religion of Baalism helped maintain this feudal structure (the word Baal means landlord). Baal was considered the supreme deity, and landlords were regarded as lesser baals—gods of lesser power and worth. At the bottom of the social and economic scale were the serfs and the slaves.

There was a natural tendency among the more aggressive Hebrews to covet the advantages which Baalism gave to the wealthy among the Canaanites, and they began to change their own religion to conform to the values of Baal worship. This change tended to transform Yahweh into a copy of Baal. Accordingly, a deep conflict developed between those who saw Yahweh as the protector of the weak (those who sought to have religion maintain its traditional *mishpat* ethics) and those who wished to remove any religious opposition to their attainment of wealth and power. The struggle against Baalism forms a common theme in all the historic books. The history of the early centuries, when the Hebrews struggled to possess the land of Canaan, focuses on this problem. A good king is one who resists the temptations of Baal; a bad king is one who throws in his lot with the innovators.

The books of Joshua, Judges, Samuel, Kings, and Chronicles tell the story of the Hebrew people over a period of five or six centuries. They narrate the invasion of the land of Canaan, and the founding of the monarchy under Kings Saul, David, and Solomon. This period in the narrative is followed by the decline of the empire, and its subsequent division under the sons of Solomon. The last books mentioned above relate the tragic history of Israel and Judah until their fall and captivity—the northern kingdom in 721 B.C. and the southern kingdom of Judah, conquered by the Babylonians in 597 B.C.

While these books contain the history of the Old Testament, they are written (particularly Joshua and Judges) in a highly imaginative way. They are filled with legends and sagas of early biblical times. They interpret victories and defeats not as effects of particular tactics but as products of the Hebrew people's faithfulness or unfaithfulness to Yahweh. Thus these books tell us that the walls of Jericho fell down before the armies of Yahweh, while the sun stood still so that Joshua might win the battle on the chosen day. The battering rams and spears that really won the battle are nowhere in evidence. Here too is the story of Gideon and his little band of three hundred outwitting and defeating the hordes of the enemy. Finally, there is the glorification of the shepherd lad, David, who with his sling vanquished the giant Goliath. The common theme in these books is the story of the struggle of Yahweh against the influence of Baalism: The true heroes are the prophets, the spokesmen of Yahweh who must teach their kings the true path to victory.

The high points of Hebrew history as related in the Bible are the reigns of King David and his son, Solomon. This era of glamor surpasses any other period—witness the visit of the Queen of Sheba with its display of wealth and power, and the great temple that was built to Yahweh in Jerusalem. During this period of consolidation, Israel traded throughout the Eastern world; but, ironically, at this same time Baalism achieved its greatest influence over the Hebrew religion. These two aspects go together.

Both David and Solomon violated some of the stricter tenets of Yahwism. For example, they married foreign wives to strengthen their alliances or open new trade routes. Such political decisions violated the injunctions so strongly laid down in the book of Deuteronomy; these acts were seen as flagrant provocations of the priestly class and the rural elements. David and Solomon promoted a strong commercial civilization whose ethics were inevitably closer to Baalism than to Yahwism. This development led to violations of *mishpat* justice, and to violations of the land holding rights of the poorer Hebrews. Consequently, the imperial successes of these two venerated kings intensified the class structure of landlordism, and imposed heavy burdens upon the poorer classes.

In his book *God and the Social Process*, Graham Wallis reveals the consequences of David's actions as he vividly points out the changes that took place during the king's lifetime. He says:

> In David's childhood, the Israelite element was purely pastoral, agricultural, and non-commercial, being identified with open villages in the country . . .and yet within the space of one lifetime, not only were the village clans organized and consolidated on a wider territorial expanse, but the political forces of the country were suddenly focused within the Amorite city of Jebus, or Jerusalem. The country shepherd lad of Bethlehem gradually became an effete, oriental monarch, dwelling within the shelter of stout city walls, influenced by his large harem, swayed by the counsels of men who were already learning to ignore the social standards of kinship groups in the open country. In short, a landowning and slaveholding aristocracy was developing under David's reign.

Yahweh was no longer seen as merely the watchful deity of nomadic tribes. During David's reign he became the exalted God of a mighty empire, who was worshipped in great temples with elaborate rituals.

Strangely enough, some of this ritual is still preserved in Christian worship. How often one hears the refrain of it in present-day churches, during the responsive reading of the 24th Psalm:

> Lift up your heads, O ye gates,
> And be ye lifted up, ye everlasting doors,

And the King of Glory will come in.
Who is this King of Glory? The Lord,
Strong and mighty, the Lord, mighty
in battle, He is the King of Glory.

However, in Hebrew culture, as in every culture, the old traditions persisted. The poor and needy still regarded Yahweh as the protector of the nation's morals and the defender of their struggle against the oppression of the mighty. It was only at this time that what Nietschze called the "morality of the weak" first developed—not as a new form of ethics but as a desperate clinging to the ancient ways of justice. Such faith kept alive the struggle for justice in Israel's life. Class struggle was seen in the revolts against David, and later against Solomon. It was also seen in the legendary struggles of Elijah and Elisha (their struggles against King Ahab and Queen Jezebel are found in 1st Kings).

We raised the question in the first part of this chapter: How does one reconcile the different conceptions of God found in the Bible? On the one hand he is a God of vengeance, and on the other he is a God of loving kindness and tender mercy. But such paradoxes are visible in every period of history—even in our own. Consider America's changing vision of the President over the past two hundred years—and then remember that the Hebrews' vision of Yahweh attempts to balance the changes of a thousand years and more.

In ancient Israel, Yahweh was first a tribal diety, demanding the utmost loyalty and obedience in order to preserve the integrity of the community. At the same time, Yahweh was seen as fiercely committed to protecting the well being of his people—even to the extent of destroying their enemies.

Later Yahweh became the national God, and finally the Great God Yahweh—the God of a great and powerful empire. But during this same period the prophets began to portray Yahweh as a universal God of justice and righteousness. All the people of the earth were included in His concern and love. This concept, given to the Hebrews by the prophets, has not ended all contention. There is always the legacy of ancient loyalties and enmities, the same loyalties and enmities that demean popular religion in all nations and times.

How was this last—and greatest—transformation of Yahweh accomplished? In the next chapter we will turn from kings to prophets, to examine the efforts of a few great individuals to change the imperial Yahweh into a universal God of love and justice. Before their struggles, all the legends of warriors fade into background.

5

The Prophets

The first books of the Old Testament to be written were those of the eighth century B.C. prophets. There were seventeen in all, comprising one fourth of the writings of the Old Testament; but the best known of these writings are the books of Amos, Hosea, Isaiah, Jeremiah and Ezekiel. It is a cast of kooks, a roster of ancient hippies and lonely demonstrators. Most of these prophets were the radicals of their day, though we should not infer therefore that all radicals are prophets! Certainly these writers were severe critics of the conventionally accepted religion of the Hebrews. Like today's radicals, they were quick to condemn outmoded, old-fashioned religious rites and traditions, and they gave short shrift to conventional arguments for the legitimacy of myths, fables and stories of miraculous happenings.

There are obvious contemporary parallels, examples of such men and women in all cultures. As in ancient Israel, people today are taught to repeat creeds which they do not understand—creeds couched in a language and a mode of thought archaic to all except philosophers and theologians. They preserve old legends and superstitions they do not analyze, and hold onto ceremonies and forms of worship that have long since lost all relevance to their ways of living. It is also true that, then as now, cruelties and injustices develop within culture. Legal forms and procedures become more important than the intentions behind them, but since they are accepted by the lay society they go unchallenged by conventional religion. This happened in the life of the Hebrews.

But, during the eighth and seventh centuries B.C., a number of men challenged the contemporary religions of Israel and Judah. Critics are never particularly welcome; these were condemned and vilified by their culture. Fortunately they survived the persecution and wrote down their insights; their lives consequently illumine the nature of the struggle which constantly goes on between conventional forms of life and the ethical insights of sensitive thinkers.

Amos—The Outside Agitator

Amos, the first of these prophets to appear, was denounced by the people of Israel as an outside agitator, and ordered to return to the land from whence he came. A citizen of the southern kingdom of Judah, Amos appeared upon the streets of the city of Bethel in the northern kingdom of Israel. It was an inauspicious time for this stranger to appear in a rival nation spouting prophecies of doom. He arrived during a great celebration of victory; the masses were rejoicing over their recent military successes. The country was enjoying a period of unusual prosperity, resulting from heavy military expenditures. They shrugged off their new taxes.

The temples were filled with joyful worshippers; celebrants knew that Yahweh was looking with favor upon them, for He had granted them victory. But to the alien, Amos, all this appeared evidence of a false faith. Amos saw that, while the people of Israel were glorying in their military power and prosperity, they were neglecting elementary justice toward the poor. There was luxury only among the privileged classes; among the poor there was oppression. As Amos phrased it in Amos 2 : 6:

> This is what the Lord says: "They have sold the righteous for a handful of silver, and the needy for a pair of shoes. They grind the faces of the poor into the dust and force the humble out of his rightful path."

Amos did not accept the popular religion. He did not

accept the traditional belief that Yahweh's function was to win battles. Instead, he saw Yahweh as the defender of the weak, and he felt called upon to reassert that *mishpat* justice which had sustained the hopes of the poor in the past.

Amos also introduced a radical new dimension to the vision of Yahweh. To him, Yahweh was the God of all nations. He directed the affairs of all, and judged Israel and its enemies alike with the same righteousness. Moreover, thought Amos, the Hebrews were not the only Chosen People, to be protected merely because of their ancestry and the ancient promises. They were chosen only so long as they deserved the choice. In Amos 9 : 7, Amos quotes Yahweh as saying:

> Are you not to me as the children of the Ethiopians, O children of Israel? Have I not brought up Israel out of the land of Egypt; And the Phillistines from Caphor, And the Syrians from Kir?

To make matters worse, Amos prophesied that Yahweh would send enemies to defeat the children of Israel because of their social injustices. The people couldn't decide if Amos was a worse traitor or heretic. All patriotic Israelis were offended for they saw their nation's God as its protection against enemies. A nation's religion, they claimed, gave it security, and the worship of Yahweh the War God acted as a guardian of law and order against those who would disturb that security.

So they called Amos a "prophet," their tongues dripping with sarcasm. He denied it, saying he was neither a priest nor a prophet. He made no pretense of authority, and instead claimed to be only a tender of sheep and a dresser of syca-more vines. He was merely one of the common people. When Amaziah, the High Priest, ordered him back to his own country, suggesting facetiously that he might be able to make his living there by prophesying, Amos replied,

> I am not a prophet, but God has taken me away from my sheep and said: 'Go prophesy to my people Israel.' You tell me not to prophesy to Israel, but I tell you your wife is going to be ravished in this city, your sons

and daughters will die by the sword, and you will die
on impure soil, when Israel goes into exile.

Amos' prediction did come true for many people of Israel,
but it took almost half a century to happen. It is a possibility which Amos might well have foreseen; however, it
seems more likely that this was added to his prophesies by a
later hand. Amos was more concerned with the present;
that was why he refused the title of prophet. His eyes were
on conditions at that time, not possible consequences.

Amos is regarded as one of the great prophets of Israel,
but we must admit that his fame is due mainly to his early
start. The Bible mentions a whole run of "prophets" who
were neither honest nor sincere. These were persons who
told the future by reading the stars, or by studying the
entrails of slain animals. There were soothsayers who pretended special powers, and witches who pretended to sum-
mon people from the past to give guidance to the worried.
Even King Saul, in a time of desperation, called upon the
witch of Endor in order to consult with the shade of the
departed Samuel. It can be readily seen that Amos' sincerity
made him stand out in his company. Indeed, some of his
best work was the exposure of quacks.

For example, those least trusted by Amos were the so-
called prophets who attached themselves to the king's
courts. They became a part of the king's retinue, serving
sycophantically to assure him of God's favor on his latest
project. It was (and remains today) a common procedure. It
has characterized the court of kings and the cabinets of
presidents or heads of states throughout history. Clark
Clifford once spoke of the tendency to become a syco-
phant-prophet in Washington. In an interview in Santa
Barbara, at the Center for the Study of Democratic Institutions, he warned:

> For many people around the President, the object is
> not to displease the President; the object is to ascertain
> what the President's view is on a certain subject so that
> it can then become their own view . . . In three admini-

strations I have watched advisors spend a great deal of time formulating arguments which will support the position that the President has already taken.

Jeb Magruder of Watergate fame has made a comment on one such counsellor: "He was one of the most persuasive men I've ever met. He could always see the way the President [Nixon] was leaning, and he could state brilliantly whatever the President wanted to hear."

Amos did not want to be with those who sought favor by accommodating the king's wishes. Nor did he want people to think he had some kind of magic powers enabling him to foretell events. Like the first prophet, Elijah, he knew that God's voice wasn't to be heard in theatrical thunders; it was the "still small voice" that carried God's word. In Amos' view, God spoke out of the events of the day. He, and any man of sense, could see that disasters were sure to come upon a nation which disregarded the clear judgment of a righteous God. It was Amos who gave immortal expression to Yahweh's judgment of the sacrificial system of the Hebrews. He passed on Yahweh's words (Amos 5 : 21):

> I hate, I despise your feasts. And I will not smell your solemn assemblies. Yea, though you offer me your burnt offerings and meal offerings, I will not accept them; neither will I regard the peace offerings of your fat beasts. Take away from me the noise of your songs; I will not hear the melody of your viols. But let justice roll as waters; And righteousness as an ever flowing stream.

Amos was but one of a number of men who stood out as dissenters in the life of Israel and Judah between 765 B.C. and 597 B.C. They attacked the same evils. Though they came from different walks of life, and though each was unique in his method and manner of demonstrating his convictions, they all sought to eliminate the abuses in the popular religion of the Hebrews. These dissenters did not change the character of life in their days, but they did leave a permanent influence upon the life of Judaism, and on the Christian movement which followed.

Hosea—The Prophet Who Married a Prostitute

Hosea was another of the prophets of Israel who demonstrated his criticism of his nation in a most unusual manner. He married a prostitute, claiming that Yahweh had ordered him to do so. Hosea claimed that God had said to him, "Go marry a faithless woman and have children from her unfaithfulness, for this land commits wholesale prostitution in forsaking the Lord" (J.B. Phillips' translation). Drama is important to radicals; this marriage was Hosea's method of dramatizing his rebuke of Israel. In Hosea's eyes, Israel was a harlot nation that had turned away from its true God, Yahweh, not for love of another god but for pure commercial gain.

As a further demonstration of God's purpose in punishing Israel, Hosea gave symbolic names to his children. The first he named Jezreel, based on a prophecy that Yahweh "would break the bow of Israel in the valley of Jezreel." His daughter he called Lo-rahmah (unpitied), for God said, "I will no more pity the house of Israel." A third child he named Lo-Ammi (not my people). The members of his family were, according to Hosea, living signs that Yahweh had turned from Israel.

Hosea's writing sometimes defies translation, and this problem has been intensified by the subsequent alterations of his editors. But shining through them is a clear appeal for greater faithfulness to Yahweh, and a recognition of Yahweh's loving kindness, nearly exhausted by the sins of Israel.

Aside from what is recorded in his book, little is known of Hosea. Where did he live? How did he earn his living? Many have questioned his unorthodox method of trying to awaken people to Yahweh's love and compassion, but none question Hosea's sincerity in such verses as: "Love I desire, and not sacrifice/And the knowledge of God, more than burnt offerings."

Those who recall the play, *Green Pastures,* may remember

Hosea as the prophet who walked back and forth before the battlements of heaven, appealing to Yahweh to give his erring people another chance while Gabriel urged God to let him sound the trumpet of doom. Hosea is a prophet who never gives up, a man possessed by a faith that—in the end—God's love will win.

Isaiah—The First Hippie?

Isaiah, one of the major prophets of the Bible, could easily be compared to one of the anti-war demonstrators of recent times. Though a young man possessing wealth and social standing, he spent three years on the streets of Jerusalem dressed in rags like a captive. He went about barefoot and half-naked, seeking in this unconventional way to dramatize the fate that threatened the people of his city. Isaiah would stand upon the streets of the city and sing a protest song—a ballad of the vineyard which brought forth wild (sour) grapes. His meaning was clear—Israel was the vineyard, and it was producing bitter fruits.

Isaiah lived and prophesied from the year 740 B.C. until the year 700 B.C. He resided in the southern kingdom of Judah, and therefore witnessed the fall of the northern kingdom, Israel. Seeing what had happened to Israel, he was surer than ever that his own nation needed to change its manner of life. But his methods differed from those of his predecessors. In contrast to both Amos and Hosea, Isaiah was a young aristocrat. He moved freely among the leaders of the community and had access to the king. Isaiah might be compared to Wendell Phillips, the wealthy and aristocratic young lawyer in Boston who threw in his lot with the anti-slavery forces in the days before the Civil War. Phillips brought bitter antagonism down on his head; his peers accused him of treason to his class. Likewise, Isaiah suffered bitter hostility from the leaders of the city of Jerusalem. Tradition has it that he was finally "sawn asunder" on the orders of the king.

For forty years Isaiah walked up and down the streets of

his city of Jerusalem, appealing to people to commit their lives in holiness to Yahweh. He urged them to establish justice in their dealings with the poor. It was a time of magnificent mansions, of large landholdings, and of splendid worship. But it was also a time when peasants were being evicted from their homes, and the shadow of war hung over the land. Isaiah prophesied that the nation would be ruined and that humiliation would be brought upon the city. As Dr. Fleming James described it,

> It was a heroic faith that the prophet demanded of the commonplace men of his times. To follow it meant to give up not only everything which clashed with Yahweh's requirements but all the measures which ordinary foresight would prescribe...No wonder that he encountered scoffers. The marvel was that he could persuade a few.[9]

In the final analysis Isaiah too was dismissed as an impossible and impractical idealist.

Isaiah did not live long enough to see the destruction and humiliation brought upon his city, but his influence was so great that it extended long beyond his lifetime. It was aided by two other writers who each added to Isaiah's prophecies. Their contributions dealt with conditions after the fall of Jerusalem. Yet another writer added some of the most famous lines attributed to Isaiah, the prediction of a redeemer who would someday deliver Jerusalem from its fate.

While Isaiah's specific appeal to the people of his own day met with derision, his universal vision of a land of peace and security has long been preserved as the poetic expression of a dream that men of all ages have hoped would some day come true. In one famous passage, Isaiah speaks of a king who will have such wisdom that the Spirit of the eternal God will come to hover over the land. He concludes with the hope of a renewed Eden:

> And the wolf shall lie down with the lamb
> And the leopard shall lie with the kid...
> And a little child shall lead them...

They shall not hurt nor destroy in all my
  holy mountain
For the earth shall be full of the knowledge of God
As the waters cover the sea.

Jeremiah—The Lonely Prophet

Jeremiah, one of the best known of the Old Testament
prophets, lived in the southern kingdom of Judah for more
than forty years (626-586 B.C.). His was a long and active
life that saw him estranged from his mother, socially ostracized, constantly threatened, and imprisoned several times.
He witnessed the destruction of Jerusalem, and shared the
subsequent exile of Jerusalem's prominent citizens to
Babylon.

Jeremiah was a successful prophet; that is, he predicted
exactly the disaster that came upon the city of Jerusalem and
the nation of Judah. He had prophesied that Yahweh would
send the Babylonians to invade the land. To dramatize his
predictions, he even appeared upon the streets with a yoke
bar upon his neck, saying, "This is what Yahweh plans for
the people of the land."

As Jeremiah had proclaimed, Yahweh gave their land to
Nebuchadnezzar; the Judeans wore the Babylonian yoke.
By the time the prediction came to pass, Jeremiah had been
denounced as a traitor and thrown into prison.

Not only was Jeremiah denounced for his dire prophesies,
but he was also berated for his severe criticism of Judah's
rulers. He denounced their failure to establish just national
and international procedures. They were responsible, he
claimed, for the growth of false worship of Baal. Jeremiah
demanded a complete reform of the nation. Speaking in the
name of Yahweh, he called upon the people:

> Amend your lives and doings that I may dwell among
> you in the temple. Never rely on false phrases like:
> "This is the Eternal's temple, his very own temple."
> If you really amend your lives and your doings, if you
> really see justice done between man and man, if you
> give up oppressing aliens, orphans and widows, give

> up shedding of innocent blood in this place and fol-
> lowing other gods to your hurt, I will allow you to
> remain in the land . . . You are relying on false phrases
> to no profit. What? Steal, murder, commit adultery,
> perjure yourself, sacrifice to Baal, and then come to
> present yourselves before me in this house . . . thinking
> you are safe, safe to go on with all those abominations?
> (Jeremiah 7 : 1)

Jeremiah's call for a thorough reformation of the Hebrew religion based on the highest moral insights had little effect. Vicious customs had become common following the introduction of foreign gods from Nineveh and Babylon. The worship of these gods led to many strange evils including the horrible rite of child sacrifice. All these practices led to a moral decline that culminated in the final destruction of the country by the Babylonians.

Appalled by the evils in his land, and saddened by the threat to its inhabitants, Jeremiah lived a lonely life. He never married. He reported that Yahweh forbade him to marry or have children. To him Yahweh had said:

> Thou shalt not take thee a wife, neither shalt thou have
> sons and daughters in this place. For thus saith Yahweh
> concerning sons and daughters born in this place . . .
> they shall die grevious deaths; they shall not be la
> mented, neither shall they be buried, they shall be a
> dung upon the face of the ground, and they shall be
> consumed by the sword, and by famine, and their
> dead bodies shall be food for the birds of the heavens
> and the beasts of the field (Jeremiah 16 : 1–4).

Whether Jeremiah actually made this prediction, out of his deep pessimism, or whether it was added after the fact by a later hand is unimportant. He ultimately witnessed such complete devastation that he may well have added this prophecy as justification for the fears that he had expressed so often or he could merely have expressed that common fear vented by many when the future seems threatening.

When the city of Jerusalem finally fell to the Babylonians, Jeremiah was given a choice. He could go into exile with the leaders, or he could remain in the destroyed city. He finally went with some of the refugees to Egypt. From there he sent encouragement and hope to his despairing people.

Though Jeremiah had threatened the destruction of his city, after the fulfillment of his threats he sought to comfort the survivors and to voice Yahweh's great love for them. He told them that though they were banished from the city they were not banished from Yahweh's presence; though their temple had been destroyed, Yahweh's presence was still in their hearts.

To Jeremiah, Yahweh did not need the Temple to be present to His worshipers. Yahweh was present wherever there were faithful hearts. This was Jeremiah's greatest contribution to the future of the Hebrew religion. Henceforth, worship was not to be tied to the Temple. Worship was to be a personal matter, and not wholly concerned with the nation's life. Thus Jeremiah made way for the building of the Tabernacle, where the people could worship and not be wholly dominated by the priests. It is a change without which Christianity could never have become the dominant religion of the West, for every Protestant denomination accepts the individual's direct link to God.

Ezekiel and Flying Saucers

Ezekiel is one prophet who gives everyone difficulties, for his prophecies are extremely complex. Scholars in the field are confused as to what his visions mean. Perhaps they were clearer to contemporaries, for his gift of hope was welcomed by the exiles when they were taken to Babylon. He shared their dispirited exile, asking with them, "How can we sing the Lord's song in a strange land?" Ezekiel spoke to his fellow sufferers; but he spoke in visions. He is the most symbolic of all the prophets.

In the first part of his book Ezekiel tells of a chariot which had wheels within wheels. He describes the creatures in it as having four faces and four wings. "Zekiel Saw De Wheels" is an American spiritual that has popularized this vision.

What Ezekiel meant by this vision, one can only speculate. He described the vision as "the appearance of the glory of the Lord." For him, perhaps it was. People often express their spiritual visions in outlandish ways.

A scientist recently asserted that Ezekiel's vision was neither more nor less than an authentic flying saucer sighting. Moreover, he concluded, Ezekiel had seen some people from outer space. The machine Ezekiel described seemed to him to be ideal not for moving from earth to heaven but for traveling through interstellar space.

Another vision Ezekiel had was of the "Valley of Dry Bones," which prompted him to ask, "Can these dry bones live?" This vision has also been immortalized in a spiritual. In the song, the bones of a skeleton are assembled one by one, then covered with flesh, becoming a living person. This process symbolized the hope which Ezekiel had for his people that a new spirit, a revival of hope and of religious zeal, might take possession of them. With this revival, they might become more eager for the path of Yahweh, and in this way bring new life to the nation.

Through these visions Ezekiel stressed the work and power of the individual, as well as his responsibility. To Ezekiel, you are not the victim of heredity; you are not liable for the transgressions of your parents. He called upon his people to repent their sins and reach a new level of existence, "Repent then, get you a new heart and a new spirit."

Dr. Edgar Goodspeed has interpreted Ezekiel as a prophet and a priest who looked forward to the rebuilding of the temple, and who sought to mold the life of his nation to follow a purer ecclesiastical control. Because of his influence in this direction, he has been called the "Father of Judaism." Certainly, after the return of the people from exile, Judaism did show a more ecclesiastical bent. Ironically, the influence of the priestly element was so strong that it became dominant in Judaism, subduing the prophetic note. What began as a celebration of the individual vision of God gradually deteriorated into the "dry bones" of the Pharisees.

Summary

Because of the unique methods of the Hebrew prophets, they have offered a pattern for subsequent prophetic individuals. I have described some of the bizarre methods which they used: going barefoot through the streets, wearing a yoke upon the neck, and marrying a prostitute. When ordinary methods fail, unusual persons seek unusual ways to call attention to their messages. In recent times we have seen unusual demonstrations, which have aroused establishment hostility.

Unfortunately, being unusual is not enough—you must *see* unusually clearly as well. A recent press story tells of a man who tried a method suggested in Luke's Gospel (12 : 3). He went upon a housetop (a tall building) to shout his message; but only his method was unusual. The report did not mention any results. In our day we have seen many youths adopting unorthodox styles of dress and hair arrangements to emphasize their rejection of the ways of their elders. Many of these youths have adopted a communal lifestyle and have turned their backs upon the lure of financial success. But it remains to be seen if they will follow up their rejection of old forms with the introduction of new substance.

While some may not equate all today's rebellious youth with the prophets of Israel and Judah, there are, nevertheless, some similarities. Like the recent protesters, the prophets were jailed and threatened with death. Similarly, some of our youth languished in jails, and thousands were prevented from returning to their homeland because of their demonstrated opposition to the Vietnam War.

The prophets of the Old Testament made some harsh criticisms of their people; in reaction, later writers edited their books. This editing was done partly to soften their criticisms and partly to express new hopes for the nation. For, with the passage of time, much of their work was accomplished; Jerusalem was rebuilt, and new prospects opened before the Hebrews. In the next chapter we shall deal with some of these new directions sought by the nation of Israel.

6

New Directions

The later period of the Hebrew nation following the reign of Solomon is not as well known as the earlier. Partly this occurs because there is an imaginative and romantic character to the stories of the prehistoric ages that is not present in more recent events. Also, early Hebrew history records a vital transformation of the known world when hope and faith spawned miracles and promise led to conquest and victory.

In contrast, the days following the exile were times of discouragement. The Hebrew people faced the task of rebuilding the city and restoring the temple. It was a time when religious zeal was at a low level, a time of pessimistic skepticism. The discouragement of the people was voiced by some of the lesser-known prophets: Malachi, Joel, and Obadiah. The great expectations that had sustained the Hebrew people during their centuries of conquest and victory had not been fulfilled. There had been a few years of greatness during the days of David and Solomon, but these conditions of wealth and glory soon passed away. As Harry Gersh states, in *The Sacred Books of the Jews,*

> In their more than three thousand years as a people, they had not been politically independent for more than a few hundred years; they had lived in their homeland for only a third of their existence, and from the days of the Judges they had been under pressure to assimilate into larger cultures, and to accept more

powerful religions. This they had refused to do.[10]

The Hebrews had fought against being assimilated by other races and religions, but they had been divided, invaded, and conquered; finally, they had been driven from their home. Those who returned from exile to the southern kingdom of Judah were, except for a very brief period, subject to the powerful nations which surrounded them. First there was Babylon, then came Egypt, and finally Macedon and Rome.

What was the future destiny of this once proud and conquering people? This was the question that faced the returning exiles. There were some who realized that they were too weak to conquer their enemies. These realists knew that they must find other ways to make the great promises of Yahweh come true. While the promises to Abraham had not been realized, they were determined to keep alive their faith and to hope for deliverance. In the meantime they would retain their chosen identity, they would not merge with other nations, their religious forms would remain uncontaminated, intermarriage would again be strictly forbidden, and the laws of Yahweh would be fully observed. The failure to observe these laws and ceremonials, especially on the part of those who had married out of the faith, had brought the punishment of destruction and exile upon the nation according to general opinion.

At this time, priestly influence fastened upon the Jewish people; the religion known as Judaism had its beginning. The priests insisted upon strict observance of the ceremonials in their worship: the sacrificial system with its altar for the burning of the sacrificial animals, the rite of circumcision, and strict Sabbath observance. This trend in the life of the nation was enhanced by the publication of the first five books of the Bible. From this time on, these writings mythically entitled the "Law of Moses" became the sacred law of the Jewish people.

The publication of these books attributed to Moses was soon followed by a book of history. It was composed of the books we know as 1st Chronicles, 2nd Chronicles, Ezra, and Nehemiah. These four books, as we now know them, are thought by scholars to have been originally one book. The books of Chronicles (The Chronicles of the Kings) cover the same material as the Book of Kings discussed in Chapter 4, but they continue the story of the nation of Judah through the days of the exile and into the time of the rebuilding of Jerusalem. They were written when the priestly influence was at its height, to retell the nation's story from that point of view.

There were, however, others among the Hebrews who were more greatly influenced by the lofty ideals and broader sympathies of the prophets than by the narrow goals of the priests. They were not concerned with ceremonial and sacrificial requirements. Moreover, these dissenters realized that although Israel could never regain its freedom by conquest, they could nevertheless erect a standard of laws, both moral and religious, that would point the way of salvation for all nations. In the deliverance of the world, Israel would obtain its own freedom. Their views have been set forth in one of the later prophecies, which was added to the earlier prophecy of Micah. This prophecy offers a superb vision of peace and security, in which all nations would one day be united by their recognition of the perfection of Yahweh's moral laws, and the sense of justice expressed in them.

> But in the end of days it shall come to pass
> That the mountain of the Lord's house shall be
> Established at the top of the mountain,
> And it shall be exalted above the hills:
> The people shall flow unto it,
> And many nations shall go up and say;
> "Come ye, and let us go to the mountain of the Lord,
> And to the house of the God of Jacob
> And he will teach us his ways
> And we shall walk in his paths."
> For out of Zion shall go forth the law,
> And the word of the Lord from Jerusalem,
> And he shall judge between many peoples,
> And they shall decide concerning mighty nations
>   afar off;

And they shall beat their swords into plowshares,
And their spears into pruning hooks;
Nation shall not lift up sword against nation,
Neither shall they learn war any more,
But they shall sit every man under his vine and fig tree;
And none shall make him afraid,
For the mouth of the Lord has spoken.
And let all peoples walk in the name of its God,
But we will walk in the name of the Lord our God
    forever and ever.
(Micah—fourth chapter)

Such prophecies opened another road for the Hebrew people and gave them hope that the prophetic insights of their religion might some day save the entire world from its warring ways.

What had happened to Micah's prophecies also happened to the writings of Isaiah. As mentioned in the last chapter, at least two other individuals added to Isaiah's writings with material that clearly derives from later times. One of these writers apparently wrote shortly after the fall of Jerusalem and another after the return of the exiles from captivity.

Isaiah, writing before the destruction of the city of Jerusalem, had voiced little hope for the country. But the later writers, seeking to bring comfort and hope to a despairing people, added more. Among these promising messages was one that has changed the course of the world—a passage called the "Messianic Hope"—the hope of a redeemer to come. This hope was a general feeling among returning exiles, expressed in various ways. Some hoped for the appearance of a good king who would restore the nation's glory and rule with justice and righteousness. Others prayed for a "Suffering Servant" who would bear in his body the sins of his people. Still another group envisioned a heavenly being who would come to earth.

These hopes had been held by various groups of Jewish people in many forms. It was (and still is) held that a redeemer will someday come to do for Jews throughout the world what Moses had done for the slaves in Egypt. Jewish people still look for the Messiah. The great twelfth century Jewish philosopher Maimonides expressed this hope often. He said once, "I believe with perfect faith in the coming of the Messiah, and though he tarry, still I believe and wait for his coming every day."

In the Christian view, the Messiah has already come in the person of Jesus of Nazareth; but even Christians rely on Isaiah's profound and beautiful prophecies in their worship. His words are incorporated into Handel's great Oratorio, "The Messiah," and sung all over the world at Christmas time: "Comfort ye, comfort ye, my people saith the Lord" and "Arise, shine, for thy light has come, and the glory of the Lord has risen upon you." One of its choruses employs the words from Isaiah expressing hope for a great king, and applies them to Jesus:

> For unto us a child is born, unto us a son is given, and the government shall be upon his shoulders, and his name shall be called Wonderful Counsellor, Mighty God, Everlasting Father, Prince of Peace.

We began this chapter by raising the question of the future course of the Jewish nation. Faced with the reconstruction of their nation they had several options; typically, they tried them all. Some, fostered and strengthened by the priestly element, looked to the past traditions of Moses. This emphasis has continued to the present day among more conservative Jews. The more liberal Jews are the inheritors of those who broke with most of the old forms. Although they preserve some ceremonial ties to the past, their emphasis has been upon the moral and ethical values contained in the prophetic portions of their past.

And there were more skeptical voices, some of them expressed in other books incorporated into the Old Testament. These solitary figures yield yet another insight into the rich development of Jewish traditions.

7

Faith and Skepticism

In the last chapter we spoke of those unknown writers who sought to revive the faith of the Hebrew people in their destiny and in the fulfillment of their faith. There were other writers who did not share the faith and hope of the leaders of that time. These writers were doubtful of the recovery of the nation's long lost glory and skeptical of promises of victory, prosperity, and long life. Their writings, usually called the Wisdom Books, include Ecclesiastes, Job and Proverbs.

Before we come to them, however, we must examine one book which appeared late in Israel's history (about 150 B.C.), but which still emphasized the traditional goals. It consists of a collection of devotional material known as the Psalms. It sums up, in poetic form, the rich promises that the Hebrew religion has always offered to those who followed Yahweh and obeyed his laws. Psalms has become one of the most treasured books of the Bible.

While these poetic expressions of faith are attributed to King David (just as centuries of laws were all attributed to Moses), many of them were actually written by other people. Appearing as a completed book only about the middle of the second century B.C., they tell a tale of longing for God's care and concern. They entreat His protection from danger within and without. The Twenty-third Psalm, for instance, has become a classic and is probably the best known of all psalms. It is known as the Shepherd Psalm, for it promises comfort and shelter to all God's children both in life and in death.

There are other psalms which make more explicit promises to those who are faithful to Yahweh. The First Psalm voices such a promise, saying, "The righteous shall be like a tree planted by the rivers of water, that yields its fruit in due season, and whatsoever he doeth shall prosper." The Thirty-seventh Psalm, similarly, opens with a long recital of all the fears which plague mankind. But there is assurance for those who trust the Lord,

> Trust in the Lord and do good; so shall
> you dwell in the land, and enjoy security.
> Take delight in the Lord and he shall give
> you the delight of your heart.

The psalmist promises more: "The wicked shall be cut off," and those "who wait upon the Lord will possess the land . . . . The meek shall possess the land and delight themselves in abundant prosperity." As testimony to God's abundant care, the psalmist asserts, "I have been young, and now I am old, yet never have I seen the righteous forsaken, nor his seed begging bread."

The Ninety-first Psalm offers protection from enemies and danger, "For He shall give His angels charge over you, to bear you up lest you dash your foot against a stone." Here too one finds the famous prediction, "You shall tread upon the lion and the adder." This same psalm ends with a promise, "With long life will I satisfy him and show him my salvation." Nowadays, the Ninety-first Psalm is used mainly by certain religious groups that handle deadly snakes in their worship services. Faith could not be tested further than this (though hospitals record many who fail this particular one).

The promises so strongly made in the Book of Psalms reflect a joy in God that fills much of the Old Testament; but there are two books in the Bible that are exceptions. These are Ecclesiastes and Job. Though they appeared about the same time the Book of Psalms was compiled, nothing could be further from that book's spirit. Professor Sandmel, of the Hebrew Union College, remarks, "Ecclesiastes is a gentle and whimsical comment on the prevailing and traditional view of religion; if a man observed the commandments, he would receive the rewards of long life, and wealth, and children." The writer of Ecclesiastes says, in effect, "This view may be true, but it is not always the case." He goes on to assert that, even if it were, the "rewards" provide only vanity and vexation of spirit.

It is important to ask who wrote the Book of Ecclesiastes, and why he wrote it. Further, why was this book—with its cynical denial of traditional religion—placed in the collection of sacred writings of the Hebrews?

The book claims to be the words of Solomon, son of David. Scholars doubt this claim and put the authorship centuries later—as late as the second century B.C. While no one has discovered who wrote the Book of Ecclesiastes, the writer clearly reflects the uncertainty of this late period of the nation's life. The author exploits the exploded confidence of the earlier period as an ironic setting for his melancholy views of life.

The author of the Book of Ecclesiastes could easily have felt that Solomon was a perfect spokesman for his lament, for that great king's wisdom, wealth, and power had led only to frustration. And certainly the actual author felt frustrated about conditions in his day. So this writer wrote a book in which he put his own melancholy views into the mouth of Solomon (referring to Solomon as "the Preacher"). He quotes Solomon, saying:

> I have been king over Israel in Jerusalem. And I have applied my mind to search out by wisdom all that is done under heaven. It is an unhappy business that God has given to the sons of men to be busy with. I have seen everything that is done under the sun; and behold, all is vanity and a striving after wind.

Solomon is further alleged to have said that he sought all the things Yahweh promised to those who kept faith with him. But once he found them, they were empty. He had tried pleasure, collected great works, built mansions, amassed silver and gold—but it was all for naught. Therefore, he concluded (according to the writer) that nothing in man's world is worthwhile. He had looked upon the evil and oppression in the world, and decided that the dead in their graves were happier than the living. Filled with bitterness, he asserted that the same fate awaits the good and the bad; the best human efforts are defeated by the rules of chance.

There are people today who ask the same questions as did the writer of Ecclesiastes. They question the promises of a half century ago: increasing wealth, abundance, and ease were supposed to be the ultimate bounties. But today, despite all our affluence and the dazzling exploits of science, our fears are more frightening than ever—our uncertainties greater. Many today ask if our fierce struggle can ever pay off. This is the question which Robert Heilbroner asks, in his *Inquiry into The Human Prospect* (Norton, 1974). He writes:

> More and more we have come to question the game: whether the game is worth the candle . . . . There's a widespread feeling, which I certainly share, that our industrial society, hooked on a diet of consumption and growth, has simply not paid off in terms of human happiness. We are, by all figures of gross national product and that sort of thing, twice as rich as our parents, four times as rich as our grandparents, and God knows how many times as rich as our Pilgrim forefathers. But nobody would claim that we're twice as well off, twice as happy, twice as fulfilled, four times better human beings than our grandparents.

We feel, with the author of Ecclesiastes, that even when new things do appear "under the sun," they don't deliver us from the old malaise. Thus, a more poignant reaction to the mood of Ecclesiastes has been seen during the last few years in the lives of many young people. They have turned away from the values of their parents in order to search for a simpler and, to them, more meaningful way of existence.

They have left their homes of comfort and luxury; they have dropped out of prestigious universities. They have ignored the mores and morals of conventional society, deliberately turning their backs upon careers that offer as their prime rewards wealth and ease, to seek happiness instead. As a rule, they are turned off by conventional religion and their parents' goals. In effect, they ask of our society the same questions as the writer of Ecclesiastes did of his. And we are not surprised, for this too the writer had anticipated: "To everything there is a season," even for the doubter. Thus, maybe it is because Ecclesiastes is a commentary on a constantly recurring mood of doubt that this book was accepted in the collection of writings known as Sacred Scripture. Even I, in my years of study, have reflected occasionally on the words he could have spoken directly to me, "Of making books there is no end."

The Drama of Job

If Ecclesiastes is a book of doubt, Job is a book almost of despair. The Book of Job is a drama attacking conventionally optimistic views. It was written about four hundred years before the time of Jesus to confront the perennial question of human suffering and ask "Why?"

Everyone knows something about the story of Job. For most of us, his name is a synonym for suffering and sorrow. He lost fortune and family, and was afflicted with excruciating torture. Being human, he cried out asking why. The conventional answer (brought by friends who are ironically called "Job's Comforters") was that he suffered because of his unfaithfulness and sin. Job's comforters, armed with all the then current arguments, tried to convince him that he was suffering as a result of his transgressions. They assured him that if he would merely confess his sins and seek forgiveness he would get relief. It was the same argument used by those who sought to turn the history of the Hebrews into a myth of moral transgressions. Job rejected this and, maintaining his innocence, decided to present his case directly to God. This conflict between conventional wisdom and individual will gives drama and greatness to the book.

The drama opens with the sons of God coming before the Lord. For some reason, Satan is also present. Seeing him there, God asks him where he came from, and Satan answers, "From wandering to and fro upon the face of the earth." Then God, wanting to display His people, asks him if he has observed His servant Job, "a man blameless and upright, who worships God and shuns evil." Satan, however, questions Job's uprightness. He taunts God, asking, "Does Job serve God for naught? Look, you've given him everything, houses and land and wealth, sons and daughters. Put forth your hand and touch all that he has, and he will curse you to your face." It is a childish dare, but God meets Satan on his immature level by putting everything in Satan's hands—with the sole admonition that he is not to touch Job's person.

Job then suffers a series of calamities: the loss of his property by an Arab attack, the loss of his houses by lightning, and the death of his children by a whirlwind. To all this Job responds as God had hoped, "The Lord giveth, the Lord taketh away, blessed be the name of the Lord."

In his next encounter with God, Satan is again questioned about God's servant Job and his faithfulness. To these questions Satan replies, "Skin for skin, all that a man has will he give for his life. Put forth your hand and touch him bone and flesh, then see how faithful he will remain." God's response is predictable; He is demonstrating the futility of questioning faith. "There," he says, "he is in your hands, only save his life." Following this interview Job is afflicted with boils over all his body.

As he sits among the ashes of his home, scraping his boil-ridden body, his wife chides him, "Still holding to your loyalty! Why don't you curse God and die?" But Job replies, "Are we to take good from the Lord, and not evil, too?" The highpoint of Job's faith comes when he asserts, "Though he slay me, yet will I trust him." With these words, Job rises to a higher faith, which acknowledges the evil and injustice in the world, but steadfastly maintains that there is a purpose to life which man serves by his faithfulness to God. It is a noble faith, which has been asserted by heroes and martyrs in all ages.

Unfortunately, the story ends with a lack of realism; Job has been restored to his position in the community, he has regained his wealth and his health, and he has more children —thus God blesses him anew. But such a happy ending fails to answer the initial question which has taunted those who feel that they suffer unjustly. Is it *necessary* for death and disaster to be brought upon Job and his family? The fact of God's almighty power is ultimately incomprehensible— and that shatters our pride even more than Ecclesiastes' assertion of our futility.

The Book of Job is perhaps the most serious book of the Bible, for it reveals people wrestling with one of the deepest philosophical questions: the nature of good and evil. In our era of random violence it is more pertinent than ever, for it is a question not only debated by theologians, philosophers, and serious playwrights, but earnestly asked by all of us.

The Book of Proverbs

Set in the middle of the Old Testament, the Book of Proverbs has been called one of the Wisdom Books. In that category, it has been associated with Ecclesiastes and Job, but it is quite different. The other two books depict a profound skepticism about the ancient and conventional religion of the Hebrews, while the Book of Proverbs is much lighter, merely presenting a series of common sense statements about life. These statements have appealed to all people of all ages and religions. The philosophy contained in the proverbs might be likened to the writings of the present-day humanists—avoiding the unanswerable, it looks at the unexamined.

This book appeared about two or three hundred years before the time of Christ, but the contents probably bring together ancient sayings which had lived in the minds of the Hebrew people over many centuries. Though it is not one of the directly skeptical books of the Old Testament, it does represent a more practical, down-to-earth attitude than is normally found in theological writings. As such its wisdom is not to be ignored.

Such writings often appear at times when theology has become rigidly dogmatic and highly speculative, or during times when men's minds have become confused over the widely differing claims of rival theologies as to the nature of the supernatural, and the ways of salvation.

In colonial America, for example, when the concept of being pioneers in a New World was still confusing to many, Benjamin Franklin wrote or gathered up a series of pithy and practical sayings and published them under the title, *Poor Richard's Almanack.* Later, in the nineteenth century when learned men were beginning to reject the theological orthodoxy of that time, Ralph Waldo Emerson wrote a series of essays on friendship, self-examination, understanding, and reason. These efforts to bring greater understanding to all in a time of ambiguity are analogous to the Book of Proverbs.

The writer of Proverbs gathered common Hebrew sayings and presented them as the voice of wisdom. He writes, "My son, be attentive to my wisdom, incline your ear to my understanding that you may keep discretion." Because of the tradition that Solomon was "the wisest of men," the proverbs are commonly attributed to him. Solomon must have been a decidedly eccentric man since his wisdom has allegedly produced the radical doubt of Ecclesiastes, the practical lessons of Proverbs, and the erotic poetry of the "Songs of Solomon"! In any case, Proverbs opens: "The proverbs of Solomon, son of David, king of Israel: that men may know wisdom and instruction in wise dealing, righteousness, justice, and equity, that prudence may be given to the simple, knowledge and discretion to youth . . .and the man of understanding acquire skill, to understand a proverb and figure the words of the wise and their riddles."

The fact that these wise proverbs were attributed to Solomon illustrates the great impact of fable and myth in the Bible, and shows further how men grow in stature over centuries of time. After all, anyone who took "seven hundred wives and three hundred mistresses" deserves some other appellation than "the wisest of men." More seriously, Solomon also demonstrated poor judgment in the ordering of his kingdom, for he let it slip into chaos and division. So much for the way that generations automatically attribute wisdom to their distant rulers.

Many of the proverbs are obscure, but some have a universal simplicity that makes them classics. The close of the book, for example, is a wonderful tribute to the faithful wife. She is pictured as more precious than jewels, and as always industrious. She serves her household and her husband with tireless effort, "looking well to the ways of her household, and eating not the bread of idleness." Such a wife is "blessed by her children and praised by her husband . . .charm is deceitful, and beauty is vain, but a woman who fears the Lord is to be praised." This praise might sound a bit old-fashioned, and I might be called a chauvinist for reproducing it, but such virtues have represented a merger of wisdom and frugality which has earned commendation over eons of time.

The proverbs of a people often seem a better guide to their fundamental character than theology. Theologies are subject to radical change, and then they cause bitter strife. Contemporary history shows that theology has too often led to conflict and wars. But human nature and human behavior do not change radically or vary from race to race. The proverbs of humanity could furnish a ground for better understanding and peace between nations. How much pain might humanity have been spared if we had heeded the lesson "Pride goeth before destruction . . . .Before honor is humility."

8

Truth in Fiction

Thus far we have been discussing works that purport to be fact, though often we've found a large measure of fiction or myth. But some of the books of the Bible are overtly fictional in character. The fact that they are does not detract from their religious value, nor does it weaken the message the writer intended. Fiction is a very powerful instrument for revealing ethical dilemmas, or for pricking the conscience of the indifferent. Dickens, for example, moved the people of England to tears when he portrayed conditions among the wretched poor. He made David Copperfield and Little Nell real people to his English contemporaries; when Nell "died," the churches were thronged with people praying for her soul. Similarly, Harriet Beecher Stowe's *Uncle Tom's Cabin* aroused a fury of opposition to slavery in America. In like manner, the biblical writers used fiction to dramatize conflicts in their society that threatened the highest ethics of the Jewish religion.

The best known fictions in the Bible were written in the latter days of the Jewish nation. Two of these stories attacked a growing racial intolerance. Another called for an heroic defense of Israel, and of Judaism as a religion. The most famous of these three writings, Jonah, has been the center of controversy for centuries—a controversy not about the story's central thesis, but about its imaginary nature. Because many people are unable to go beyond their doctrine of biblical "truth," they have argued for literal and absolute truth in this obviously fantastic story, rather than seeing it in its proper perspective of spiritual truth, symbolically rendered. You may think that serious theologians do not labor under such misapprehensions; in that case you should know that recently the students and faculty of a large Lutheran Seminary were required to declare publicly their belief that the story of Jonah was literally factual. Many quit the seminary and organized another, where such a drain on their credulity would not be demanded.

The Book of Jonah tells the story of a man who was thrown overboard during a storm at sea. He was swallowed by a big fish. People usually speak of Jonah being swallowed by a whale, but the writer only called it "a big fish." Here, as elsewhere in the Bible, the influence of its translation has disguised the precise language of the original. As the story tells it, Jonah lived for three days in the belly of the fish. Then he was literally thrown up on the shores of Nineveh to tell his fantastic story.

Clearly, the purpose of the story of Jonah was not to demonstrate that God could make a fish large enough to swallow a man (and furnish him adequate quarters for a cruise). This spectacular element in Jonah's tale has only a minor function in a more serious and more obvious purpose. Jonah is the unwilling instrument of God, delegated to carry a message of friendship and reconciliation to a hated enemy. He is a draftee, a reluctant, conscripted internationalist. He is ordered to go to Nineveh and to call upon the people there to repent so that they might be saved. Jonah does not want to do it, for he shares his people's hatred for the people of Nineveh. So great was this hatred in Jerusalem that one of the prophets, Nahum, once wrote a hymn of hate directed at the wicked city. Such ill will had been intensified in Jonah's time by the fact that many of the people of Jerusalem were held captive in Nineveh.

To avoid the commission which has been given to him, Jonah seeks to escape by taking a ship going in the opposite direction. It is during this voyage that God raises a storm to foil Jonah's escape. The incident of the fish merely shows to what lengths God will go to save His people from their own weakness.

The story ends with Jonah carrying out the orders of Yahweh, pronouncing doom upon the city of Nineveh. Then the story reaches its true climax: the people of Nineveh do what Jonah did not want them to do—they repent. This disturbs Jonah, since the last thing he wanted was for Nineveh to be saved; but *that* had been God's purpose all along.

The story ends with God's rebuke to Jonah. He asks Jonah, "Am I not to be sorry for this great city of Nineveh with its hundred and twenty thousands of infants who know not their right hand from their left?" God's question is a pertinent one for today's leaders, now that the vivid memory of our Vietnam atrocities is only beginning to be balanced by a new concern for human rights throughout the world—even among our "sworn enemies."

Ruth—A Racial Love Story

The story of Ruth is another bit of historical fiction, dealing with the same general theme faced by the writer of Jonah. This story has often been referred to as one of the gems of Hebrew literature. We quote its ending in wedding ceremonies, but the part that reads, "Entreat me not to leave you, or to turn back from following me, for where you go, I will go . . . your people shall be my people, and your God, my God," somehow has never seemed fitting to me. Those who know my concern with reading the Bible in its fullest context will understand why. The text of this quote is the plea of a young widow that she be allowed to accompany her mother-in-law back to her own land, and to share her life with her. It is made against the advice of the older woman, who fears the prejudices Ruth will face because she comes from another land and race. This sentiment and desire, beautiful as it is, does not fit a wedding ceremony, though its relevance to our newly-proud minority groups lends it added power in that context.

Ruth reflects the strong racial feelings in the time following the exile, though from fear of censure, the writer, like the writer of the story of Jonah, set the scene in a conveniently distant time (some eight hundred years before the time of writing). The writer's purpose was to counteract in a small way the growing racial intolerance in the life of the nation at the time of his writing.

The story of Ruth begins with a man from Bethlehem who, with his wife and two sons, moves into the land of the Moabites. There the man dies and his two sons marry native women. After the two sons die, Naomi, their mother, decides to return to her native land. The two daughters-in-law want to accompany her, but she tries to dissuade them. One does go back, but the other, Ruth, persists until Naomi agrees to take her. Clearly, this story represents a common situation: Moabite women, even though married to Hebrew husbands, remain foreigners in the eyes of Naomi and others; she foresees the great difficulties and prejudices they would face if they tried to enter Israel.

The reason for such prejudice is not hard to find; Moab bordered the land of the Hebrews, and there was fierce enmity in the land of Israel toward the Moabites. Intermarriage was fiercely condemned because it gave Moab claims on Israeli territory. Naomi herself may have harbored such prejudices. At best, she felt that her daughters-in-law would be happier in their own land.

The focus of the story is Ruth's persistence; she does accompany her mother-in-law. She is then befriended by and later married to Boaz, a rich brother of her father-in-law. It is a vital merger for the Hebrews, for one of Ruth's descendants is the most revered of the kings of Israel, David. Through this reminder of genealogical history, the writer brings a strong indictment against the wave of intolerance that during the first years after the exile was sweeping his land.

Who wrote the story?—we do not know. It was written sometime after the year 400 B.C., that much is certain.

There is little confirmed fact in this legend, but it is possible that the lingering tradition of a Moabite strain in David's ancestry lay behind the tale. Certainly the story of Ruth served its purpose: it has combatted narrow attitudes toward the people of other lands ever since its composition.

Esther—Never Underestimate the Power of a Woman

One might wonder why the story of Esther found its way into the collection of Hebrew religious writings; it seems to have no particular religious value. But it is part of Jewish folklore; it is good for an embattled people to have the story of a clever woman who outwitted the enemies of her people.

The story comes from the time of the Jewish exile in Persia. Steeped in Persian intrigue, plots and counter plots, reminiscent of Asiatic tales rather than most biblical stories, the Book of Esther tells of a beautiful young woman who thwarted the vicious desires of her captors. Furthermore, the incident described gave rise to the Feast of Purim, one of Judaism's few completely happy holidays.

The story is of course a bit of romantic fiction. It has even been suggested that it might be an adaptation of a Babylonian legend. But whatever its derivation, it would make credible television fare today: the young girl saves her virtue and her father's life with a single stroke.

Esther is introduced as one of the young women who have been summoned to appear before King Xerxes (in the story known by the name of Ahasuerus), to see who will replace Queen Vashti, whom he has deposed. As the story proceeds, Esther finds favor with the king and is made queen. In that position she performs great services for her captive countrymen, and she is the pivotal character in a series of attempted assassinations of her husband and counter assassinations plotted against Hebrew leaders. Mordecai, one of these leaders and Esther's adoptive father, is in special disfavor with the king's counsellors. Haman, the villain of the story, obtains a decree from the king demanding that all men should prostrate themselves before the king. Haman knows that Mordecai's religion will not let him do this and foresees a quick end to this thorn in his side.

At this point, Esther does a daring thing: she appears before the king without having been summoned. This was an offense which traditionally called for death, even for the queen. But the king welcomes her and, charmed by her beauty, offers her anything she desires. Esther asks to be allowed to give a dinner for the court and expressly asks that Haman be present. In the meantime, the king is bothered with insomnia and, in the midst of his sleepless thoughts, recalls how Mordecai once saved his life. The next morning he demands to know what has been done to reward Mordecai. Finding that nothing has been done, he orders Haman to dress Mordecai in royal clothes, adorn him with a crown, and give him one of the king's horses. Haman is, as you might imagine, crushed by these favors to his rival.

In the denouement of the story, the tables are turned against Haman. Esther reveals the plot which Haman had devised against Mordecai and all her people. Haman is subsequently hanged on the very gallows he had prepared for Mordecai, and in turn the Jews destroy Haman's sons and followers. Here a bit of wish fulfillment comes in, as the writer describes the small bands of Jews going out and killing some seventy-five thousand of their enemies—with the king's sanction!

In a sticky ending, Mordecai winds up as chief counsellor to the king. He is honored among both Jews and non-Jews. He is respected for his zealous regard for the welfare of his people and for his role as peacemaker. Both Mordecai and Esther remain Jewish folk heroes, for this story is one of the few places in the Bible where plain old adventure and power politics are the only focus. There are no laws and no lessons; only a good boost to the ego.

Daniel Had Clout

In the second century B.C., historic forces met in a bitter struggle over Judea. The year was 165 B.C., and the combatants were the Jews and the armies of Antiochus IV, King of Syria. Israel, with its tradition of proud parochialism, found itself challenged by the growing, more universal spirit of Hellenism, and she determined to "fight rather than switch." Israel swore to keep Judaism protected from the influences of other cultures, fearing (with good reason) the loss of its traditions and beliefs.

When Alexander's forces had swept over that part of the world some one hundred and fifty years before, Alexander had left behind a vision of a universal faith that would bring unity, peace and understanding. This was the beginning of the Hellenism which so threatened the Jews. Alexander's early death in 323 B.C. cut short his political efforts, but the vision persisted. It was the vision of humanity united by a common appreciation of reason, distilled in Alexander by his childhood tutor, Aristotle.

The conflict between Judaism and Hellenism has been described by Arnold Toynbee as a conflict between two noble ideals. Both faiths, says Toynbee, saw themselves as struggling for universal acceptance, but—as happens so often in history—these philosophies which sought to universalize themselves through political forces found themselves in bloody conflict.

When Antiochus IV, acting under this Hellenic impulse, tried to wipe out the Jewish faith, the Jews rose in rebellion. The Syrian king tried to stamp out the ceremonies in the temple; he bribed people to profane the Sabbath and to pollute the sanctuary. The Jews were, he said, to build altars and shrines to pagan idols, cease practicing circumcision, and forget their obsolete laws. He warned that to disobey was to court death.

It is no wonder that the Jews rose up in one of the bloodiest rebellions of their history. Amid this climate of desperate circumstances the writer of the Book of Daniel composed his tale of a similar crisis in Hebrew history, four hundred years before. He told of the time when the Jews' faith was being tested by King Nebuchadnezzar in Babylon. To gain a sympathetic focus for his book, the author took as his hero a lad by the name of Daniel.

The writer of the Book of Daniel did for the people of Jerusalem in 165 B.C. what the composer Verdi did for the Italian people in 1865. In Verdi's time the Italian people chafed under the Austrian yoke and were struggling toward their climactic revolution finally won in 1871. So, in patriotic fervor, Verdi took the story of Daniel and composed around it the opera *Nabucco*. His symbolic purpose was achieved; the opera gave his people hope and encouragement to continue their fight against oppression.

Neither the writer of the Book of Daniel nor the composer Verdi dared to write directly about the problems which their people faced. For either to do so would have resulted in accusations of treason. Therefore, they resorted to the thin disguise of historical analogy.

In the biblical story, Daniel and his Hebrew friends are captives in Babylon. They have attracted the attention of the king, through the superior quality of their faith and their virtuous conduct. But the king's advisors, hostile to these subversive Hebrews, have Daniel's three companions thrown into a fiery furnace, and Daniel sealed up in a lion's den. Through their faith they all escape unharmed. The king is overjoyed, and he revenges himself upon his faithless advisors. He then rewards Daniel and his companions by elevating them to positions of influence.

Throughout this highly imaginative story runs an account of Daniel's gift at interpreting dreams, and of his prophecies concerning the fall of kingdoms. Ostensibly, he predicts the fall of the Babylonian, Medean, and Macedonian Empires. Actually, the empires had fallen long after the time of Daniel (remember, the story is written with perfect hindsight), but the author invoked literary license to put into Daniel's mouth these prophecies. With this device the writer encouraged his readers to wait a little longer for the end of their tyrant's career since, after all, Daniel's dreams had come true—how could theirs fail?

Dr. Herbert Willett comments about the Book of Daniel:

> The influence of Daniel has been widespread and profound. The fact that the faith of the Jewish community was kept alive through times of deep distress was due to the combined effects of the Maccabean revolution and the reading of this book. It has remained through the centuries one of the favorite portions of the Jewish Scripture. So much of a classic did it become after the crisis of the Syrian persecution had passed, it retained its popularity and served to prepare its readers for other emergencies in the later days, e.g. the Roman wars of A.D. 60–70.[11]

It is fitting that, with an analysis of the book which played the greatest part in stiffening the Jews against the double pressure of Rome and Christianity, we end our examination of the Old Testament. We have seen how these sacred books shared by three religions were composed, through a fusion of factual knowledge, fictional genius, and fantastic mythmaking over the course of two thousand years. In the space of a single century, Jewish resistance would be overcome, leaving the Hebrews a relatively tiny remnant of a process that ultimately changed the entire world. Without understanding Hebrew history, we could not understand either the present thoughts of Jews in Israel and around the world, or the incredible metamorphosis that took place two thousand years ago. It is time to turn to Jesus.

9

The New Testament

The New Testament writings were produced by members of a new religious movement which developed after the death of Jesus of Nazareth, as he was known during his short life. The movement would later become the Christian Church.

This movement, formed by the first followers of Jesus, took many forms and developed many differing interpretations. The disciples never fully understood Jesus' purpose when he was alive, and this confusion was heightened by the tragedy of his death. In the decades following the Crucifixion, many groups formed in different parts of the Roman Empire. These separate groups developed conflicting theologies about Jesus, as well as differing modes of worship and behavior.

During the century following the death of Jesus, a collection of writings was produced which later became known as the New Testament. The first of these writings to be produced were the letters of Paul. Later there appeared letters attributed to John, to Peter, and to Jude. All these letters deal with problems facing any new movement in religion. Another book appeared soon after, which deals largely with the events in the life of Paul and was written by Luke, known as Acts of the Apostles. Then, among the last of the books to be written were the four books called Gospels. These contain all the extant records, legends, traditions and interpretations of the life of Jesus. Finally, the collection closes with a cryptically prophetic book known as the Revelation of John. In the early centuries of the Church's life, these writings of the New Testament, along with those of the Old Testament, were accepted as the authorized body of sacred literature, "the Word of God."

The books of the New Testament developed out of events in the life of the early Church. Without the Church there would have been no New Testament, and no Gospel stories about Jesus. Long after the Church had been organized, the writers of the four Gospels realized that such a far-flung movement needed some central body of truth to counter the growing influence of oral tradition. They thus began to recover the accounts of Jesus' life, gathering them from scanty records and memories, as well as from traditions which had been embellished over the decades.

As the events of Jesus' life receded into the past, imagination enlarged on them, and writers interpreted them according to the various faiths and viewpoints which had developed in each individual church. If the Church was to grow, doctrines had to be formulated and questions answered concerning the precise nature of Jesus. How was he related to God? Was he the Messiah sent to save the Hebrew nation? There were also many unanswered questions about his death and Resurrection.

During these early decades there was little interest in the daily life of Jesus. The early Church simply believed that Jesus would soon return to earth and set up his kingdom. By the time interest had developed about the earthly life of Jesus based on the growing realization that he would not return right away, he was already a transcendent figure surrounded by legend and fantasy. The stories in the written Gospels were thus to a large degree interpretations of legends —interpretations which were bound to vary among the four. We must always bear in mind this important fact: the New Testament is fundamentally based on interpretations of Jesus, rather than on factual accounts of his life.

In connection with the above observation, we should notice that winsome and appealing stories have emerged about Jesus throughout subsequent history. It should be noted that Mark's Gospel, which is considered the one based on the earliest traditions, has the least flavor of the miraculous in its interpretation. It has none of those appealing stories clustering around the birth of Jesus, the stories of shepherds and of the chorus of angels. When this Gospel was written, these stories had probably not developed in the eager and adoring minds of the early disciples. In the later Gospels of Matthew and Luke, they do appear, showing how important it is to distinguish between history and myth in the Bible.

In even later times there were other writings—much more fanciful and less appealing—which have not been admitted to the collection of recognized Sacred Scripture. In a collection known as the *Apocryphal New Testament* (published in Oxford by the Clarendon Press) we can find many such stories. For example, there is a tale of Jesus turning a group of children into goats and then turning them back into children at the request of their parents, who became his devoted followers. In another story of this early Christian period, we find Jesus modeling clay pigeons, turning them loose, and watching them fly away.

Clever storytellers throughout the ages have fashioned tales designed to cast a spell of belief and create a mood of devotion towards Jesus. In Europe, during the Middle Ages, they told the story of oxen who knelt at midnight on Christmas Eve. Even as late as the nineteenth century, Tolstoi wrote the appealing story "Where Love Is, God Is," which imagines how Jesus could come to life today.

If this tendency to fantasize about Jesus has continued through the centuries, it was certainly active in the time of heightened speculation and eager hopes which marked the days after Jesus' Crucifixion. The Jewish people, who constituted the largest proportion of the Christian Church during the early days, were deeply concerned with the question of whether Jesus was the Messiah. This was the basic question that the author of Matthew's Gospel sought to satisfy. Later, when Paul started churches among the Gentiles, people trained in a Greek or Hellenic manner of thought, he had to present a different focus; he therefore gives a different interpretation of Jesus in his writings.

Clearly, this short survey of the circumstances surrounding the writing of the New Testament shows that its composition was in large part a reaction to the development of the Church. We can think of these writings as an effort to accomplish something the Hebrews had never tried: the creation of a worldwide network of faith, linked not by physical proximity but merely by the Book itself.

Since it was through the Church that the New Testament began, we cannot help but ask, how did the Church get started? There is no sure answer, so we are reduced to relying on what records we do have. These records, with the help of a little imagination, will allow us to reconstruct the events which followed the execution of Jesus.

The reports of these events given in the Gospels and in the Book of Acts reflect the disciples' various visions, which were not recorded until decades later. They differ widely, show liberal doses of imagination, and are difficult to evaluate.

The main problem is that, while the events of the trial and Crucifixion of Jesus occupy a central place in the traditions of the Church and in Christian theology, they apparently did not create much of a stir in Jerusalem. Such happenings took place almost every day in A.D. 33. Rome feared revolutionary movements and moved quickly to execute rebel leaders; Jesus was considered as just another rebel by the authorities. Thus, there is hardly any mention of the death of Jesus in the secular histories of the time, which might lead one to conclude that the importance of these events has been greatly overstated by the Gospel stories, as well as by Christian theology. The Crucifixion was, however, a terrible human tragedy in the lives of Jesus' small group of disciples; such shattering personal events could not be too greatly magnified.

As reconstructed from the legends recorded in the Gospel stories, Jesus awakened great hopes in the minds of his disciples. He promised a new kingdom of justice and righteousness on earth. They did not understand all that he had taught them, but he inspired their undying love and loyalty. They were not prepared for such a brutal ending to their dreams. Their hopes were dashed. In the records we have, produced from tradition, we learn that the disciples were frightened and confused; they fled the scene. In the first days after the Crucifixion, the disciples acted just like the rabble the Romans thought them to be.

But after their understandable terror had subsided, the disciples returned to Jerusalem. They came back to share their memories, and to compare reactions to the tales that had sprung up. The strongest of these rumors was that Jesus was alive—that he had risen from the dead! Some of the group claimed to have seen him. There were fantastic stories of Jesus appearing to his disciples, only to mysteriously disappear from their sight. One such appearance occurred to two of his disciples as they walked along the road towards Emmaus. They did not recognize him until they broke bread together; he chided them for forgetting him so soon, then disappeared as suddenly as he had come.

One story, preserved in the first chapter of Acts, gives a vivid account of Jesus being lifted upon a cloud away from the sight of the apostles. He left them only a promise that he would return in a like manner. This story has kept Christians' expectations alive for two thousand years. From time to time, believing the day has come, small groups ascend hillsides to await Jesus' return.

The rumors that Jesus was alive and that he had appeared to his disciples formed the basis of the faith of the early Christians. Such stories lifted the mood of despair surrounding the disciples. To them, Jesus was alive; he would soon return to set up his kingdom. That was all they needed to know.

Thus, the Christian Church began among the disciples of Jesus, who met in secret out of fear of the authorities and shared their hopes for the future. When they met, they would talk about Jesus' preachings and discuss how to prepare for his return.

So strong was the common bond of fellowship among the early Christians that, according to the Book of Acts, the members held everything in common. As it is recorded in the fourth chapter of that book,

> Now there was but one heart and soul among the multitudes of the believers; not one of them considered anything his personal property, they shared all they had with one another. There was not one needy person among them, for those who owned land or houses sold them, and brought the proceeds of the sale, laying the money at the feet of the apostles; it was then distributed to each of the members according to his needs.

Some people believe that, despite his avowed atheism, Karl Marx drew upon the Bible when he came to state one of the cardinal principles of his *Communist Manifesto*. Of course, such arrangement sometimes didn't work out among the early Christians. The fifth chapter of Acts records that one man, Ananias, held back some of his money. Ananias sold his property, but lied about the amount he received. When confronted with his deceit, the story is that he fell dead. His wife, who had been a partner in his deceit, suffered the same fate. As a result of this incident, the name Ananias has become a synonym for liar.

How long the followers of Jesus attempted to practice a religiously motivated communism is not known, but the tradition has been very strong at many times during Christian history. Religious and secular groups often withdraw into communal forms of life when faced with difficult times or hostile environments; there is something quite attractive in the self-sufficient wholeness of such groups. According to one tradition, Jesus himself may have belonged to a communal group, the Essenes. Certainly many such groups existed during Jesus' day, a circumstance well documented in the Dead Sea Scrolls.

Doubtless the main influence supporting the Christians' communal life was their faith in the imminent return of Jesus. People reasoned that if Jesus were soon to return and set up his kingdom, there was no need to save or amass property. They would have all the security they needed in the new kingdom set up by their Master. Indeed, Albert Schweitzer attributed all the extreme teachings of Jesus recorded in the Gospels (e.g., "give to him that asketh, and turn not away") to the expectation of his return in the near future.

But, as this serene confidence in Jesus' return receded into the background, other problems and questions confronted the new movement. If Jesus were not to return soon, what was to be the nature of their organization? Who would exercise authority? How would the organization be held together without the presence of their leader? What was to be the basis of membership in the churches? Who would be admitted?

The above questions developed strains within and between the churches. Each group answered them differently. Contrary to the naive belief of many today who profess a longing for the simple faith of the early Church, things did not go smoothly even in those days. There were conflicts and breaches disturbingly similar to those between present-day denominations.

In looking back over the meager accounts left to us, what stands out as a major factor is the number of leaders seeking preeminence over each church. In the church in Corinth there were several schisms, and each group chose a different leader. Prospective leaders claimed to be followers of Paul or of Peter; still others claimed to follow Apollos. Paul wrote to the quarreling leaders urging them to drop their partisanship and center their affection in Christ. But in the absence of agreement as to what exactly Jesus had taught, this effort at peacemaking was not notably successful.

One of the sharpest breaks that developed among the early churches was that between the church in Jerusalem and the churches organized by Paul. The Jerusalem church was probably the first church organized after the death of Jesus, and it was headed by two leaders with impeccable credentials: James, the brother of Jesus, and Peter, Jesus' appointed "rock." The Jerusalem church was conservative, being composed of converted Jews who recognized Jesus as the Messiah but maintained most of their Jewish traditions. Later, when Paul came along with his doctrine of freedom from the old Jewish laws, a profound disagreement arose over the future role of the Church, which we must reserve for fuller treatment in the next chapter.

One new direction involved an exciting event recorded in the early chapters of Acts—an event which many Christian churches take to be the birthday of the Church. As the story has been told by Luke, thousands of people gathered together on the day of Pentecost. The Holy Spirit descended upon this gathering and empowered the people to go out and speak powerfully in Jesus' name. As described in Acts, "tongues as of fire" stood out on the heads of the people, and they spoke in a multitude of languages. People from all parts of the world could thus hear the Gospel in their own tongue. At the time, skeptics dismissed the phenomenon, saying that the people "were brimful of new wine." But Peter defended the custom, saying to the congregation, "These men are not drunk; why it is only nine in the morning." He asserted that such a happening had been prophesied in the Old Testament by Joel, who had said that in the last days, "I [God] will pour out my spirit upon all flesh . . . Your sons and daughters will prophesy, your young men shall see visions, and your old men shall dream dreams." This vivid scene, described by Luke in the Book of Acts, has inspired some churches (right up to the present day) to try to reenact such demonstrations in their worship services. James Baldwin described such a Pentecostal service in his autobiographical first novel, *Go Tell it On the Mountain*.

In the beginning of this chapter, I suggested that in order to reconstruct the beginnings of the Church we must combine the few records we have with a dash of imagination. It seems that this is what Luke himself did with his accounts in Acts, for Paul's letters seem to discount any highly demonstrative method of witnessing to the presence of the spirit (see 1st Cor 13). In his letter to the Galatians, Paul wrote, "The fruits of the spirit are love, joy, peace, patience, kindness, goodness, faithfulness, *gentleness, self-control* [emphasis mine]."

From the evidence, then, it would seem that the Church really began in the manner we described at the outset of this chapter—that is, with quiet meetings among the disciples. They met in memory of Jesus, and in contemplation of his teachings. The nature of the fellowship that Jesus created accords best with such loving conversations, rather than with the noisy demonstrations at Pentecost described by Luke.

10

Paul the Radical

As previously noted, the first books of the New Testament to be written were the letters of Paul. From this fact we can conclude that the Church was widely organized, both among the Jews in Judea and among the Gentiles in many parts of the Roman Empire, before there were any New Testament writings.

Paul was the most dynamic leader of the early Christian churches. He visited the major cities of the Roman Empire organizing churches and preaching the new faith. As he moved from one city to another, he wrote letters to previously visited churches; these letters were preserved and later became a large part of the collection now known as the New Testament.

Some of Paul's letters can be dated fairly accurately. The first one was written about the middle of the first century after Christ. Paul wrote a warm greeting to the church which he had founded at Thessalonika, expressing his deep joy at the faithfulness of the church members. They had, he said, stood firm in the face of criticism and opposition on the part of their neighbors. Paul also counseled them on their questions concerning the early return of Jesus.

Paul later wrote a second letter to the same church, dealing with its members' reaction to the promised return of Jesus. Some of the members of the church had ceased working. Why continue at their tasks, they reasoned, when Jesus would soon return and set up his kingdom? These members' fatalistic attitudes created resentment within the church and in the larger community, for they placed a burden on the rest of the members and set a poor example to possible converts. Paul strongly urged the idle to return to their duties and suggested that those who would not work should not eat. These two letters, with their warm personal tone of appreciation and their strong admonitions, form the beginnings of the New Testament. They set the tone for all the writings to follow.

Paul's letters are useful for many reasons. They explain Paul's personal faith, they develop his public theology about Jesus, and they deal with practical problems of church organization which included inevitable disputes and quarrels. One of Paul's letters to the Galatians is a sharp polemic in defense of his actions—actions which were markedly different from those of the leading Jerusalem church, and which thus drew fire from conservative elements. It is doubtful whether the Church would ever have grown as it did without the personal example and continual guidance of a man like Paul.

For it is vital to understand the situation that prevailed in the early days of the religious movement following the death of Jesus. After Jesus had been put to death, grave differences of opinion and serious unresolved questions surfaced among the disciples. They differed about what he had taught them. They raised significant questions about him. Was he the Messiah who had been promised to the Jews? If he were the Messiah, why had God permitted him to be put to death at the hands of wicked men? Was he the divine Son of God? Most importantly, had he planned to start a new Church, or merely to reform Judaism? This last position was the one held by the members of the church at Jerusalem and was the one Paul had to address most often. Differences became sharper after Paul entered the ranks of the followers of Jesus. Bitter feelings concerning these questions developed between Paul, on the one hand, and

Peter and James, on the other.

The original disciples distrusted Paul for many reasons. He had not come into the Christian movement until a decade or two after the death of Jesus; he had not known Jesus when he was alive. Indeed, as a prominent leader of the conservative Jews, he had originally been a hostile opponent to all that Jesus represented; he had seen the faith expressed by Jesus as a radical break with established Judaism. In one of his writings Paul spoke of himself as having been a Pharisee of the Pharisees. He meant that he had been one of the strongest supporters of Judaism and the laws of Moses as the way of salvation for the world. He had never accepted Jesus as the Messiah of the Jews, and he had shared the provincial doubt of other Jewish leaders that anything good could come out of Nazareth. It was a common doubt; Nazareth was in Galilee, and Galilee was known as a center of disaffection and revolution. From Galilee, troublemakers often filtered into Jerusalem where they threatened the established order. Paul had also been a violent opponent of the movement formed by those who followed Jesus. His violent bent saw him take both passive and active roles in the persecution of Jesus' followers. Paul had, for example, stood by and encouraged a group of Jews to stone to death a young Christian by the name of Stephen.

But shortly after this terrible act, while Paul was on his way to Damascus to participate in further persecution of Christians, he had the experience so dramatically told in the ninth chapter of Acts. He was blinded by a great light, and knocked to the ground. There Jesus spoke to him, chiding him for his opposition, and called him to be a disciple. Paul's experience on the road to Damascus turned him around and started him in the opposite direction. Only a few days afterwards, he startled his Jewish listeners by proclaiming his newfound faith in Jesus.

After his conversion, Paul worked and studied in Judea for a number of years, and then became an apostle to the Gentiles. He had very little contact with the disciples in

Jerusalem, not only because he disagreed with them over the future of the Church, but also because he claimed that Jesus had appeared to him directly and had commissioned him to be an apostle on his own terms.

Because of this past, Paul was distrusted by both the Jewish establishment and the original leaders of the Christian Church. The Jews considered him a traitor to his own early faith and to his own people. Wherever he went the Pharisees stirred up trouble for him. They instigated riots and controversies which caused him to be imprisoned and beaten many times. At the same time, the Christians distrusted him because he had not come into the movement through the influence of the original disciples. They feared he might be a stoolpigeon for the Roman authorities.

I cannot emphasize too strongly the fact that the members of the earliest churches were Jews. During the early decades of the church, until the fall of Jerusalem in A.D. 70, all fifteen bishops of the Jerusalem church were circumcised Jews of the ancient tradition. The members of the Christian churches were attracted to Jesus, but they clung at the same time to their former Jewish traditions and customs. Ingrained in them was the concept that as Jews they were the Chosen People, and that salvation would come to the world through the Jewish law. They accepted Jesus as the Messiah, but they believed that he had come specifically to the Jews, that he was *their* Messiah. If non-Jews wanted to enter into this fellowship, they would first have to submit to the rite of circumcision and become Jews. These early Christians did not envision any radical break with Jewish law. For a time, Paul was a solitary figure in his personal form of faith.

When Paul became a follower of Jesus, he made a complete break with Jewish law. He became an apostle to the Gentiles because he recognized that the Gentiles had no emotional ties with Jewish law nor any intention of becoming Jews. In fact, the Gentiles expressed no interest in the hopes of salvation through a Jewish Messiah. They were more interested in the appeal of the Roman mystery religions, or in the sublimity of Hellenic philosophy. Jesus' religion appealed to them because Paul presented it as one where a divine spirit could enter into their very being and infuse them with the power to overcome their evil tendencies.

Paul's rejection of Jewish law in order to appeal to the Gentiles was difficult to take for those Jewish-Christians who still had emotional ties with their traditions. Paul's preaching sounded like anarchy; it was just too radical for the Jewish-Christians. It sounded as if Paul were saying, "We need no laws or regulations. Let everyone do as he wishes."

This position taken by Paul, known as "freedom from the law," might be better understood if we consider how later proponents have stated the principle. St. Augustine, for instance, counseled people "to love God, and do as you please." Muriel Lester, a well-known social worker in London, was once asked for the rules governing conduct in the social settlement house over which she presided. She said, "There are no rules," and then she added Augustine's words. The proponents of such a position believe that if people lived nobly and unselfishly with a genuine concern for others they would need no restrictions or compulsion of law. The Jews and the Jewish-Christians of Paul's time could not conceive how society could be held together without laws. To them, the laws of Moses were the laws of God, and righteousness was attained only by keeping these laws. Paul's innovation belies the skeptical belief of Ecclesiastes, discussed in Chapter 7, that "there is nothing new under the sun."

The main thrust of Paul's argument was that the spirit in Christ evokes a response of love and joy that frees the believer from the meticulous rituals of Jewish law. Arnold Toynbee attributes Paul's success directly to this universalism and asserts that his clear teachings were crucial in enabling Christianity to move out of its restrictive Jewish bonds.

Paul asserted that, indeed, some of the restrictions of

Jewish law violated Jesus' spirit of love. For example, one provision forbade Jews to eat with Gentiles. Paul was disturbed to see this restriction observed by Jewish-Christians —even by Peter when he visited Paul in Antioch. The controversy which Paul had with Peter over this matter is revealed in Paul's letter to the Galatians. In telling of his encounter with Peter, Paul said, "I withstood him to his face."

The law forbidding Jews to eat with Gentiles may originally have arisen because of the strict kosher regulations, but it later became a function of more than mere dietary provisions. Breaking bread together has been a problem separating most races and religions. It raises barriers between religions, social classes and races. Some churches even prohibit their members from sharing the communion meal with those of other faiths. They contend that to share in this sacrament would imply acceptance of the validity of another's faith. This near-universal custom has been hard to eradicate, even among those who try to follow Jesus' teachings about brotherhood.

Some of Paul's injunctions have suffered a similar fate of undue extension. In one controversial letter dealing with behavior in the church, Paul is quoted as admonishing women to keep silent in the churches. This advice has been grossly misinterpreted and has caused much criticism of Paul as well as much controversy. It has been used by churches, even down to the present time, as a basis for banning the ordination of women to the priesthood. This is but one example of how a too-slavish dependence upon some simple verse or admonition has twisted what was originally a piece of plain common sense and courtesy.

The simple explanation of Paul's remark is that in Paul's time women were not as well educated as men. Not comprehending what the preacher was saying, they would inevitably ask each other for interpretation, causing a hubbub. Paul's suggestion was that they wait until they were home and then ask their husbands. Paul (rightfully or foolishly) assumed that the husbands could explain!

Another problem that Paul encountered in his work with the early churches was caused by people who had been influenced by the Pentecostal custom of "speaking in tongues." In Paul's churches, some of the members caused great disturbances by their insistence on this kind of religious zeal. Paul admonished them, saying, "Let me show you a better way." This was Paul's introduction to his great poem on love. He went on to contrast noisy demonstrations to the genuineness of a life which quietly expresses the quality of love. He said:

> Though I speak with the tongues of men and of angels, and have not love, I am a noisy gong, or a clanging cymbal.

He went on to describe the quality of a life which takes precedence over prophecy and described love as being

> very patient, very kind. Love knows no jealousy; love makes no parade, gives itself no airs, is never rude, never selfish, never irritated, never resentful; love is never glad when others go wrong, love is gladdened by goodness, always slow to expose, always eager to believe the best, always hopeful, always patient. Love never disappears.

Despite such loving and profound advice, Paul has not been universally popular with all Christians. For example, many women have resented Paul's attitude toward women and marriage. They resent those passages in which he says, "Wives, obey your husbands," "Be subject to your husbands in all things," and "The husband is the head of the house." These words have strengthened opposition to equal rights for women among those who tend to exploit single quotations without regard for the total context. Again, in the same letter, Paul admonishes slaves to obey their masters. On the strength of this one line, which will be explained further in the chapter on Philemon, Paul became a figure of hatred among those who were forced to endure the bonds of slavery.

The above remarks underscore the ways in which Paul's

teachings differ from the simpler views of Jesus. Paul *does* differ from Jesus. In fact, the differences are so significant that some scholars claim that Paul gave the Church a second Gospel—the Gospel *about Jesus,* rather that the Gospel *of Jesus.* This question is the subject of the next chapter.

11

Paul or Jesus?

From the historical record analyzed above, it is clear that without Paul there would have been no worldwide Christian movement following the death of Jesus. On the strength of the evidence, the movement which began with the disciples of Jesus would have ended as a small sect within Judaism. As a direct result of Paul's work, the Christian Church became a worldwide religion.

The points on which Paul differed from Jesus were crucial in shaping the progress and program of the Christian movement. These differences are most marked in the question of the role of authority and the doctrine of salvation. In both these areas the approach of Jesus was simpler and more direct, which made his presentation more easily understood, while Paul's approach was more tradition-bound and therefore more open to abuse.

The issue of authority has always been a bone of contention between Church and State. The potential for conflict is vividly seen in the controversy over the rights of conscientious objectors in war times. The authority of conscience (interpreted as the will of God) has repeatedly confronted the absolute authority of the State. There are thousands of young men still living in Canada because their consciences would not let them fight in Vietnam, but their neighbors asserted the opposing right of the State.

Jesus answered the question of authority quite simply.

To the man who raised the question of taxation, he replied, "Render unto Caesar the things that are Caesar's, and to God the things that are God's" (Matt. 22 : 21). The answer was simple, but it was not conclusive. Who is to draw the boundary between God's domain and Caesar's? If it is to be the individual (as Jesus would have declared), what is to ensure the individual's honesty?

Thus, in contrast to Jesus' answer, Paul (in Romans 13) gives the authority of government absolute priority. He writes that there is no authority except that from God, and therefore, "He who resists the authority of the State, resists what God has appointed." The translation by J.B. Phillips produces an even more ominous reading, "Every Christian ought to obey the civil authorities, for all legitimate authority is derived from God's authority. To oppose authority is to oppose God, and such opposition is bound to be punished." What a treasured quote this has been for churches that claim absolute authority and for rulers who claim the divine right of kings!

Many people contend that Paul betrayed the revolutionary thrust in Jesus' teachings. These critics point to Jesus' scathing denunciation of those who sit in seats of power (Matt. 23 : 6), and his establishment of a pattern for revolt against such authority. They remind you that Jesus actually led a revolt against the rulers, through the demonstrations of the first Palm Sunday.

It is logical to ask how Paul, after his conversion, became in turn such a strong opponent of the legal requirements of the Jewish religion, and later such a strong advocate of existing authority. When we look at the circumstances of Paul's later life, we can understand the influences leading to these apparent contradictions. As the years went by, Paul came more and more to depend upon Roman law for security and protection. He was a Roman citizen and proud of it. Because of that citizenship, he was able to appeal to Caesar to guarantee his safety in conflicts with his enemies, and he drew comfort from Rome's demonstrated ability to assure order throughout its vast dominions. Paul saw that Rome was tolerant of the many religions in its empire so long as they did not threaten the security of the State and wisely took advantage of his status to spread the faith. Basically, Paul recognized that the authority of the State could often be useful to Christianity, and he was willing to return the compliment so long as it didn't threaten any basic tenets of Christianity.

In addition, Paul often found strong authority to be helpful in dealing with jealousy among church members. In his letters he often exercised his authority over difficult persons and situations. The letters to his young friend and co-worker, Timothy, demonstrate his use of authority, as he details methods for dealing with troublesome bishops and deacons, and advises Timothy how best to help needy widows (1st Timothy). In Paul's mind, the individual can afford to give way to authority so long as the Church profits. Only when the Church began to abuse its authority, a thousand years later, did questions arise about Paul's stance.

The second ground of contention between Paul and Jesus is the question of salvation. Jesus gave this simple response to a query about salvation from a lawyer, "Love the Lord your God with all your heart, mind, and soul, and your neighbor as yourself." There was no doctrine in this response, just a moral and spiritual challenge. Jesus challenged his followers to live a life of faith, and implied that faith is merely a product of trust—one is to trust one's Heavenly Father in the same way a child learns to trust a loving parent. For as Jesus said, "the Heavenly Father knows (as does an earthly father) how to give good gifts to his children."

While Paul expressed many of these same qualities of faith in his writings, his faith includes the acceptance of what Jesus had done for sinful humanity. His doctrine of "Salvation or Justification by Faith" has a quality of legalism about it. If we accept as fact that Christ died on the cross for our sins, we are, according to Paul, justified by our faith. Jesus' death enabled God to forgive us all, but only if we accept in turn the sacrifice made on our behalf.

Paul's doctrine of "Justification by Faith" has become in turn one of the central doctrines of the Protestant churches. In Paul's case, this interpretation grew out of his earlier experience in Judaism. As a young man, he had sought to achieve a sense of righteousness by faithfully keeping all the precepts of Jewish law. After his conversion, he seemed to find a greater peace in the acceptance of Christ's sacrifice on the cross—a sacrifice made on his behalf.

During the Reformation, Luther had an experience similar to Paul's. In his early religious life he sought a sense of salvation by keeping the rules and by following the system of penance laid down by the Catholic Church. But he found this method to be empty of joy. He finally found his peace through Paul's doctrine that "the just shall live by faith."

Because in Paul's complex series of statements there seems to be an uncompromising contrast between salvation by faith, and salvation by works (good deeds of love and kindness), yet another problem has arisen. This misunderstanding has gotten to the point where some have assumed that it doesn't really matter what a person does, so long as he has faith. Such an abuse of Christianity has helped persons, nations, and religious organizations invoke a superficial justification for shedding blood in the name of Christ. "Kill a Commie for Christ" has been on the lips of many—too many.

Paul's doctrine of salvation was strengthened by his innovations in the ritual of baptism. When performing this rite, he would immerse the entire body, calling it "Being buried with Christ in baptism." The suggestion is that the sinner has died and been buried, and then is raised a new person, with a new faith and purpose. In this ritual Paul may have been influenced by the mystery religions prevalent in Greek and Roman circles which offered members participation in the life of their gods. The initiatory rites of the mystery religions were secret and akin to those of present-day fraternal orders. Initiation was supposed to elicit deeper group loyalty. In New Testament times there were many of these mystery religions serving the symbolic and emotional needs of the Gentiles.

Paul's use of baptism and his new interpretation of the original ritual gave him greater influence with Gentiles. Shirley Jackson Case noted an interesting scriptural basis for the Roman Catholic Mass in his book *Highways of Christian Doctrine:*

> There is no doubt of the fact that Paul tremendously enhanced the prestige of Christ among the common people of Corinth when he allowed them to believe that baptism in the name of Christ inseparably united them to their savior, that they participated in his blood and body at the celebration of the Lord's Supper, that he dwelt in their bodies as a spiritual presence requiring moral purity—and that they were the "body of Christ and severally members thereof."[12]

Of course, the present-day reader of the expositions of Paul who compares them with the simpler teachings of Jesus and finds them somewhat overdone needs to remind himself that when Paul was preaching and writing very little was actually known about Jesus. While the traditions were growing up about Jesus and his teachings, people had little choice but to think of him as Paul described him, "the central figure in a mystery."

After this attempt to understand the involved views of Paul, it is a relief to turn to the emphatic simplicity of James' Epistle in the New Testament. Sharply at odds with Paul's view that faith is of more importance than works, the writer asks, "Now what use is it, my brothers, for a man to say that he has faith if his actions do not correspond with it? Could that kind of faith save anyone's soul?" The writer of this epistle (scholars doubt that it was James, for the writing reveals too much acquaintance with Greek thought and too little reverence for Jewish law to fit the leader of the Jerusalem church) went on to suggest a practical application for the ideal Christian:

> If a fellow man or a woman has no clothes to wear or

> nothing to eat, and one of you says "good luck to you" and yet gives nothing to meet their physical needs, what on earth is the good of that?...You say you have faith and I merely have good actions. Well, all you can do is show me a faith without corresponding actions, but I can show you by my actions that I have faith as well.

The letter of James is really a sermon, with a thoroughly modern tone quite in line with the present-day "social gospel." It even sometimes has a satiric bite, as when James writes:

> Go to, you rich men, weep and howl over your impending miseries. You have been storing up treasure ...but your wealth is rotting...see the wages you have defrauded. Your workmen who mowed your fields call out, and the cries of the harvesters have reached the ears of the Lord of Hosts.

The Epistle of James chides the members of the Church for catering to the well-dressed while they ignore or push aside the poor and needy. James warns them that God has chosen the poor of this world to be rich in faith, and he condemns the rich for their haughty and overbearing ways.

At the beginning of the chapter, I noted that over the centuries people have held widely differing views about the nature of the Christian life and its doctrines. I have tried to clarify some of the differences found in the writings and utterances of the leading preachers of early Christianity, for it is these first tentative formulations that have led to the greatest debate and controversy in our modern Christian churches.

12

The Runaway Slave

To those today who are disturbed by the many sharp disagreements among the various bodies of the Christian Church, or between factions within the same local congregation, Paul's letter to Philemon may make vivid the nature of a problem that has been with the Church from its very beginning.

During the past few years these differences have become very sharp. Many Presbyterian congregations have suffered strained relations between different groups over issues such as whether to allocate funds for the defense of Angela Davis. The Vietnam War of course intruded into many churches, causing heated debate. Issues such as open housing and civil rights have threatened to split some churches apart.

Paul's letter dealing with the problem of a runaway slave shows us how the first Christians handled questions of conscience. In Paul's time it was against the law to harbor a fugitive. The law is the same today—only the fugitive is different. Suppose, for example, that a close member of your family, a son or a brother, had been a fugitive draft resister at the time of the Vietnam War. Ask yourself, "Would I have harbored him? Would I have given him aid and comfort?" Compound your problem by assuming that you, like most of us, were ambivalent about the war—you thought, perhaps, that the theory behind this war was acceptable but the war itself just didn't seem right. What would you have done? Now, further complicate your dilemma by pretending that the fugitive is not kin, but only an acquaintance. This is the dimension of the problem confronting Paul.

Such an incident illustrates a recurring problem in all of life: How do we apply the spirit of love in all areas of life, or, as a philosopher might put it, how do we translate love into ethics? Such questions vividly illustrate how the greatest New Testament writings emerged out of actual situations that the Church encountered.

Philemon was a slave-owning member of one of the early Christian churches. He had come under the influence of Paul and had converted to the Christian faith under his instruction. Slave-owning does not seem right to us today. Certainly we do not consider it to be Christian. But in Paul's day, when nations went to war and defeated the enemy, the victors brought home their captives and made slaves of them. Some of the slaves did hard menial household work; some were bound to the oars of ships. The lucky ones were educated by their owners, and as cultured persons they worked as secretaries or managers of their owners' estates. Slavery was an accepted part of economic and social life. There were a few people who objected, but most people saw no reason to protest slavery even though it may have seemed cruel and unjust. The alternative, after all, was to kill all prisoners outright immediately after the battle; such severity has its precedent—consider Henry V's order to kill the French prisoners in Shakespeare's play.

We do not know what Paul's attitude was toward slavery. Certainly he never spoke out directly against the practice. He may have felt, as did many Christians of the time, that Jesus would return and set up a kingdom where all wrongs would be righted. Paul did say, however, that there "is neither Jew nor Greek, slave or free, but we are all one in Christ." However, he also said, "Slaves, obey your masters." How do we explain this contrast?

In one of his books, Howard Thurman tells the story of

his grandmother, who had been a slave in her girlhood. She was very devout and loved to have her grandson read to her from the Bible. But when once he started to read from one of Paul's letters, she stopped him, saying, "Not that!" She had memories of preachers coming to the slave quarters when she was a girl, to read and preach from the Bible. Invariably they would quote from Paul's words the injunction for slaves to obey their masters. This had deeply offended her, as well it might, and she could not bear to hear any of Paul's letters from that time on.

Paul's letter was occasioned by the fact that one of Philemon's slaves had run away from his master; it was even alleged that he had taken some of his master's possessions. Had he been captured, he would have been treated cruelly. The slave, named Onesimus, traveled to Rome where he met Paul in a Roman prison. Paul convinced Onesimus to become a member of the Christian community, and the escaped slave showed his devotion to Paul by ministering to him in prison in many helpful ways.

We do not know exactly what happened next. Possibly Onesimus decided to go back and set things straight with his master. Or he may have been like today's draft exiles—perhaps he wanted to be free from fear of the law. Paul seems to have thought that Onesimus should return on the assumption that Philemon, a Christian and a friend of Paul, would deal with his repentant slave in a kindly way—even possibly by setting him free. Paul does not make this clear in the letters; we can only guess at his thinking. At any rate, Onesimus did go back, and he took with him the letter which we find in the New Testament.

In this missive Paul tells Philemon that he is sending Onesimus back to him; however this time he comes not as a slave, but as a brother. He asks Philemon to receive Onesimus as he, Philemon, would receive Paul—as a brother in the Christian fellowship. He also adds, knowing that Onesimus had probably taken some property from Philemon when he left, that if Onesimus had wronged his master, or if he owed anything to Philemon when he left, to charge it to Paul's account. He then puts added pressure on Philemon: He reminds him of his own religious debt. We do not know the outcome of this series of events. There is, however, a tradition that Onesimus was indeed given his freedom, and that later he became a bishop in the Church. While this tradition is unconfirmed by facts, it is pleasant to dream that it might be true.

Whatever the outcome, the importance of this case of the runaway slave lies in its demonstration of the overriding concern Paul and most early Christians had with putting a sense of love into all their dealings. Sometimes their efforts caused intolerable strains—Paul had to compromise his belief in authority, Philemon had to accept the loss of his property—but throughout these struggles we can see an earnest desire for the fullest justice. That desire and the methodology of compromise helps us—two thousand years later—in making our own moral decisions.

13

The Gospel Enigma

With the New Testament letters, written out of the early Church's struggle to determine its future, we complete our discussion of the first stage of Christianity. Paul and James were instrumental in shaping the Church. But as time passed and memories faded or shifted, Christians became less and less aware of the foundation of their faith. They were losing Jesus. So, some forty years after the Crucifixion, a series of four books began to appear.

These four books, prominently placed at the beginning of the New Testament, are the Gospels of Matthew, Mark, Luke and John. They are generally accepted as the writings of these four men, who were prominent in the life of Jesus and in that of the early Church. But except for one of the Gospels (Luke), such authorship is questioned by most New Testament scholars. It is agreed that the Gospel of Luke is the work of Luke, a Greek physician who was a companion of Paul on his missionary journeys. (Luke also wrote the Acts of the Apostles, which tells of Paul's life and experiences.) The other three Gospels, however, are thought to be the work of authors who wrote decades after the time of Matthew, Mark, and John. These Gospels are the reconstructions of Jesus, not his observed portrait.

"Gospel" means good news. In the New Testament, it means the good news of Jesus. The Gospels, as previously suggested, are not factual accounts of the life of Jesus. Rather, they are interpretations of Jesus' history. The Gospels were written many decades after the time of Jesus (one was written after the end of the first century), and they depended on hand-me-down stories and legends.

By the time Luke wrote his Gospel, there were many extant books about Jesus, none of which seemed to satisfy Luke—at least this is what he indicated in his own book. In the preamble he wrote:

> Inasmuch as a number of writers have undertaken to draw up a narrative of the established facts of our religion, exactly as they have been handed down to us by the original eye witnesses . . .and inasmuch as I have gone over them carefully . . .I have decided to write them in order . . .to know the solid truth of what you have been taught.

While Luke attempted to get all the facts, he was still dependent upon common sources for his material. From the text, we can infer that Luke went back to source material apparently first written by both Mark and Matthew. So it is with them that we must start.

Mark was a nephew of Peter; one of the important traditions of the early Church is that Mark was with Peter in the latter days of his uncle's life. Traveling along with Peter, he recorded events of Jesus' life which Peter alone could have observed. These notes of Peter's reminiscences collected by Mark have been called by researching scholars Ur-Marcus (early Mark), and they apparently furnished the narrative portions not only of his own Gospel but also those of Matthew and Luke. This assumption is substantiated by the fact that of the 661 verses which make up the Gospel of Mark, 606 are exactly reproduced in Matthew, and 320 in Luke.

Tradition also had it that Matthew wrote down some of the original sayings of Jesus. He is credited with furnishing the major portion of the Sermon on the Mount as found in his fifth, sixth, and seventh chapters. However, scholars assume that rather than being the words of a single sermon they are probably a collection of random sayings of Jesus which were jotted down by Matthew at various times and finally synthesized in one great whole.

In Luke's Gospel these sayings are repeated, though there are some variations which illustrate the differences in emphasis of these two Gospel writers. In Matthew, the Beatitudes open with the words, "Blessed are the poor in spirit," whereas Luke asserts, "Blessed are the poor." The distinction between Jesus as minister to the soul and to the body runs through most of these sayings. Where Matthew speaks of those who hunger and thirst after righteousness, Luke says, "Blessed are you that hunger now, for you will be satisfied." Luke adds a warning to those who are rich and well-nourished now, admonishing them that they have had their consolation; a day of hunger will someday come to them too. Luke was always more sensitive to the needs of the poor and closer to the revolutionary outlook than the Jew Matthew. In these differences between the final editions of Luke's and Matthew's Gospels, Luke seems nearer to the source, Matthew nearer to the first church. This speculation is borne out by the fact that the final edition of Matthew dates from much later than that of Luke.

Each of the Gospels has a distinctive point of view, for there were differences in the way these four members of the early Church looked upon Jesus. The Gospel of Matthew, for instance, was written primarily for Jews. He hoped to convince them that Jesus was their promised Messiah. He quotes Jesus as saying, "I came only to the lost sheep of the house of Israel." Hence Matthew's Gospel makes constant reference to Old Testament Scriptures, pointing out that certain events had happened specifically in order to fulfill the scriptural references to the Messiah. His Gospel has been characterized as a "reformed" and "heightened" Judaism. Matthew's Gospel would have appealed to the early Jerusalem church, which felt that Jesus was attempting a reform of Judaism rather than a creation of a new religion.

The Gospel of Mark is the shortest of the Gospels. It is thought to be but an expansion of his original notes, and it therefore represents the earliest traditions of the Christian movement. There is one striking difference: Mark has no account of the Resurrection. Was the original ending of Mark lost? Or is the Resurrection a late addition to the myth of Jesus?

The writers of the Gospels of Mark and of Luke, in contrast to that of Matthew, apparently were conscious of the fact that the Christian movement had been taken over in large part by Gentiles, who were not particularly interested in the Jewish hopes of a Messiah. The authors of these two books wrote to Paul's converts, people who were more Greek or Hellenic than Hebrew.

Additionally, the writers of the Gospel of Mark and of the Gospel of Luke view Jesus as a man of his times, concerned with helping people and establishing the kingdom of God on earth. Mark gives us no stories of a miraculous birth, no genealogies intended to establish Jesus as the promised descendant of King David. Mark's Gospel merely opens with Jesus joining the radical movement of John the Baptist—an observation that gives us insight into Mark's orientation. To Mark, Jesus began and ended as the great social revolutionary.

In A.D. 30 John the Baptist was the person most feared by the Roman governors. John the Baptist had been living the life of an ascetic. He lived far from the city, over by the river Jordan. Here he preached the overthrow of the existing order of things, urging people to change their manner of living and prompting them to deal fairly and honestly with their fellow men. He chided the Jews (who claimed a special distinction and protection because they were the children of Abraham), saying to them that God could raise up children of Abraham out of the stones—given God's creative power, His past choice of the Jews could easily be annulled.

As for the governors of Judea, John the Baptist recklessly called King Herod to terms for unlawfully marrying his brother's wife; Herod eventually had him beheaded to stop his voice of justice. Later, when Herod heard of Jesus, he was most fearful that Jesus might be John the Baptist come back to life. Mark emphasizes Jesus' revolutionary kinship with John the Baptist throughout his writings.

Although Luke was Greek, not Jewish like Mark, he also stressed the wide humane sympathies of Jesus toward the poor and outcast, and he expressed Jesus' universal concern for people of other races and religions. In Luke's Gospel are found three of the most significant parables of Jesus: the parable of the prodigal son, the parable of the good Samaritan, and the parable of the Last Judgment. These parables contain the core of Jesus' message for Luke.

In the parable of the prodigal son, Jesus tells a simple story that depicts God as an understanding, kind, and forgiving father. With the Samaritan, Jesus exalts the hated foreigner as capable of showing more concern and love for his enemy than convention-ridden Jewish religious leaders. In the parable of the Last Judgment, Jesus tells of his concern for the hungry, the sick and the imprisoned: "Inasmuch as you have done it unto one of the least of these, you have done it unto me."

Despite frequent differences in content and emphasis, the first three Gospels have been called synoptic Gospels. They look at Jesus from much the same point of view, and to a large degree they use the same sources (the Gospel of John is different, as we will discuss later). Matthew, Mark, and Luke all present Jesus as a man who walked the roadways of his native land, bringing a message of hope and joy to all he met. They agree that Jesus' message focused on living without fear and with confidence in God's goodness.

As portrayed in the synoptic Gospels, Jesus sought to set people free from the rigid legalism of the conventional religion of the Jews. He urged his followers to live joyous lives of trust, exhibit love and concern for each other, share their worldly possessions, forgive their enemies, and carry no resentments. He set human beings at the center of his concern, claiming that each individual's well-being was more important than the strict demands of religious ritual or the rigid observance of Sabbath restrictions. For Jesus, the kingdom of heaven is right here, in each person's fullest existence. It is within—an innocent childlike quality that responds eagerly to truth and to love.

The reception of Jesus' teachings by his listeners was greatly influenced by the presence and domination of Rome. Its soldiers were on all the roadways and they were the universal objects of hatred to Jewish people and Gentiles alike. Certainly the presence of the Romans made Jesus' dictum to "love thine enemies" much more relevant to his people, though it made him that much more objectionable to the nationalists among them. Roman rule was, in fact, the basis for Jesus' oft-quoted saying about "going the second mile," for any Roman soldier was by law allowed to commandeer a Jewish civilian to carry his pack for him for a mile. Here as elsewhere Jesus transforms burdens into tests of faith, making life fuller for all.

Jesus was aware of the work of the radical activists who most objected to these sayings. They were the Zealots, who advocated overthrowing the Romans by force. Two from this group joined themselves to Jesus' group of disciples. He called them the "Sons of Thunder." Their views presented an interesting contrast with his own; where he advocated overcoming evil with goodness, they opted for violence. This contrast between Jesus and many who would otherwise have followed him may have been the reason why the patriotic Jewish crowd shouted for Barabbas instead of Jesus when they were offered the choice of which prisoner was to be released. Barabbas, after all, was not just a thief—he was a well-known insurrectionist against Rome.

While there is no evidence that Jesus was in any sense a Zealot, he did lead a demonstration against the temple in Jerusalem on Palm Sunday. He was critical of formal religious ceremonies that lacked any individual meaning and detested sacrifices that enhanced the power of the priests at the expense of the poor. This made it easy for the Sadducees to accuse Jesus of being a danger to Roman rule. The

Romans may have been tolerant of the Jewish religion, but they were quick to react to any signs of disorder that might lead to chaos and thence to rebellion.

According to the Gospel stories, the Pharisees were also critical of Jesus. For them, Jesus was too free, too unregimented, and too "unreligious." They, of course, were meticulous in their observance of religious forms and ceremonies. They were strict in their tithes and zealous in their faith. They carried devotion to the law to such lengths that they attacked Jesus for healing the sick on the Sabbath! In turn, Jesus chided them for being so meticulous in tithing that they failed to live by the spirit of charity that supposedly lay behind the tithe system.

The Gospel account shows Jesus as being very severe in his denunciation of the Pharisees (Matthew 23). He called them blind leaders of the blind, hypocrites and a brood of vipers. He likened them to whitewashed tombs: clean and pure without, rotten within. Later writers have felt that the Gospel writers were unfair to the Pharisees; they were not actually so bad as they were depicted, so making "Pharisee" synonomous with insincerity and dishonesty did them a disservice. They did yeoman service for Judaism between the time of the Maccabean rebellion and the destruction of Jerusalem in A.D. 70.

The Pharisees, in fact, included the leading citizens of their communities; they lived exemplary lives. Arnold Toynbee describes them as having the great virtues of sincerity, disinterestedness, wholeheartedness, and a readiness to expose themselves for the sake of the law. Toynbee explains part of their hostility to Jesus as a fear of aggressive radicalism from the notorious Galileans. As defenders of the status quo, they naturally objected to the young, unreferenced Jesus "speaking as one with authority." By contrast, any self-respecting Pharisee would not have ventured a differing opinion on any subject without first checking it with the authorities to see if all agreed. Seen in a kindly light, the Pharisees were people who put their emphasis on law and order, conventional behavior, and strong church loyalty. They failed, however, to see how these practices related to less fortunate people or to the less worthy aspects of their society.

Seen in this way, the Pharisees were not far different from traditionally religious people in our own day—those who believe that conventional morality, obedience to the laws, and faithfulness to the Church are the way to save society from its decay and difficulties. Today's Pharisees contend that any act that stresses the unjust conditions in society, without equal praise for the good, is destructive of order and unity in the Church and in America. Undue emphasis on these evils, they feel, tends to destroy the effectiveness of the Church in preaching salvation. Moreover, they often truly believe that the Gospel does not apply to social issues; in their view, religion is self-contained.

On the other hand, some studies of the Pharisees regard them in an altogether different and better light. An article in the *Union Seminary Quarterly* by Ellis Rifkin, a professor at the Hebrew Union College, presents arguments to show that the Pharisees were actually the liberals during the period preceding the coming of Jesus. According to Rifkin, the Pharisees differed from the stricter Sadducees by attempting to break the hold of the entrenched priesthood. He asserts that this effort occurred following the acceptance of the Pentateuch, around the fourth century before Christ. These original Pharisees held that the law did not stop with Moses, but that there was a living relationship between man and God, who directed the lives of the people through prophetic revelation. Rifkin adds support to a statement made a number of years ago by Rabbi Joseph Klausner, who said, "The Pharisees were more concerned with discussions of man's relations to God than with the other (the moral and ethical), because the latter seemed to them more self-evident and simple."[13]

However you interpret the basic status of the Pharisees, the Gospels tell us that many of them saw in Jesus a threat to the Jewish establishment. Jesus was described as one who taught not as a scribe but as one having authority. By custom the scribes were the official interpreters of the law, and in general they were committed to the letter of the law. Jesus, on the other hand, observed that keeping the strict letter of the law killed the free working of God's Spirit in the human heart and mind. In Jesus' case at least, the Pharisees appeared in what is far from an ideal state. No matter what their other virtues, they were incapable of appreciating Jesus' lessons.

Jesus recognized, for example, that extreme demands by organized religion often led to vicious exploitation of the poor. In order to make one's sacrifice in the temple, one had to purchase the object to be sacrificed. This had to be done with the temple coin that could only be obtained at a high rate of exchange. The money changers, Pharisees all, were in part the cause of the demonstration that occurred when Jesus entered Jerusalem on the day we now commemorate as Palm Sunday. These same events ultimately led to the arrest, trial, and Crucifixion of Jesus.

14

Interpretations of Jesus

The last chapter dealt with the portrait of Jesus given in the synoptic Gospels. But this is not the only Jesus we see in the New Testament, even though it is the one we carry with us most of the time. The history of Christianity is filled with confusion, controversy, war, and massacre, much of it occasioned by sharply differing interpretations of the nature and teachings of Jesus. In the most extreme case, Hitler reinterpreted Jesus as a Syrian in order to reconcile his liking for Christ with his hatred of Jews! There are indeed grounds for different interpretations of Jesus to be found in the various writings of the New Testament. In the last chapter we discussed the similar points of view found in the first three Gospels, but even these Gospels often differed in their interpretation of the nature of Jesus.

In contrast with the synoptic Gospels, the Gospel of John, the Epistles of John, and the Book of Hebrews differ markedly. These differences flow from later theological interpretations of Jesus. For example, certain later traditions viewed Jesus as existing above the human scene as a kind of exalted, heavenly, or divine being who was sent from heaven as a sacrifice for the sins of the world (in line with the Jewish sacrificial system). In this tradition we have the Gospel of John.

The Gospel of John

John's Gospel, written more than a hundred years after Jesus' birth, was influenced by two major changes unknown to Matthew, Mark, and Luke: the dispersion of the Jews following the destruction of Jerusalem in A.D. 70, and the rejection of Jesus by the Jewish establishment. Add to these influences the fact that the leadership of the emerging Christian Church had passed into the hands of Gentiles, and the reader can see the complexity of the times that affected this Gospel writer.

The Gospel of John is a complicated piece, which has been labeled by some as being blatantly anti-Jewish. The writer seems to use the term "Jew" in a way which leaves the impression that all Jews were hostile to Jesus. As we have seen, that was not true. Aside from the immediate disciples, there were many Jews who followed Jesus. In fact, for decades after the death of Jesus, the leaders of the new movement were Jews. There was opposition to Jesus from some Jews, but this opposition was largely restricted to the entrenched establishment.

If this distinction between the Jewish people and the Jewish establishment had been borne in mind during the past two thousand years, we would perhaps have been saved the brutalizing effects of anti–Semitism. Unfortunately, many Christians (including the writer of the Gospel of John) have accepted the unfounded accusation that the Jews as a people killed Jesus.

The anti–Semitic emphasis in the Gospel of John has been denied by some of the later biblical scholars. But whether true or not, such prejudice can be easily understood in the light of the time of the writing of this Gospel (the very latter part of the first century). Its author could look back over more than a half-century of harassment, and even persecution, of the developing Christian groups by mobs of Jewish people. One of these groups was led by Saul of Tarsus before he converted to Christianity and took the name Paul.

The opposition of the Jews to the Christians can likewise

be easily understood, for the Christians were considered as traitors to their own sacred traditions and laws. This attitude was voiced in a short story in the third chapter of the Gospel of John. It is the story of Nicodemus, a ruler of the Jews, who came to visit Jesus one night.

There are some things we don't know about this story—for instance, *why* Nicodemus came at night, or *what* he talked about. It appears that the storyteller, writing years after the event might have occurred, wanted to compare the position of organized Judaism with the views of the Christian Church of his own time. Further evidence indicates that the story of Nicodemus comes from the pen of the writer of John since the story is not told in any of the earlier Gospels. The only other time Nicodemus is mentioned in the Bible is in a later chapter of John where he and Joseph of Arimathaea appear to annoint and bury the body of Jesus.

But, to continue with the story of Nicodemus' visit to Jesus, we have to imagine what a high official might wish to say to Jesus, who at that time was at the height of his ministry in Jerusalem. Being concerned with the safety of the Jews and with the need for good order in the city, perhaps Nicodemus was worried by reports that Jesus was stirring up trouble. He might have questioned Jesus as to why he had deserted the faith of his fathers and the respect for the ancient and revered laws of the Hebrews. Whatever it was that Nicodemus wanted to know, the writer of John records this answer from Jesus, "Nicodemus, you need to be born again." This answer astonished Nicodemus and it has puzzled people ever since. What the writer of John's Gospel meant we do not know. But from Paul's interpretation, and from the tenor of John's Gospel, it seems that the writer meant for Jesus to say, "Nicodemus, you need to be born again, to become alert and alive to the ever-present Spirit of love and grace, the ever-present Spirit of God leading you into the new demands of His living Spirit. All truth and moral insight are not contained in the old laws passed down from our revered fathers of the past."

A similar spirit is evident in Jesus' farewell message to his disciples, as depicted in the fourteenth chapter of the Gospel of John. Jesus is portrayed as saying to his disciples and friends, "I must leave you now . . .but I will not leave you comfortless; I will send you another comforter, even the Spirit of truth, He will guide you into all truth."

No one knows who wrote the Gospel of John. It has been attributed to Jesus's disciple John, but most scholars disagree with this assumption. They point out that the writing in this Gospel reflects a later philosophical and theological point of view, and certainly does not reflect Jesus' own time (which John of course shared).

Whoever the writer was, he interpreted Jesus in the prevailing thought forms of the Greek world. The opening verse, for instance, speaks of Jesus as "the Word of God." This is a translation from the Greek, "the Logos of God." The translation of Logos into "Word" is considered an imperfect translation, but seemingly there is no English word which adequately expresses its meaning. Rather than "Word" we might say "the creative spirit of the universe," or "the Spirit of God which dwells in the world." This is a tremendous change from the practical here-and-now style of the other apostles.

Dr. Moffatt has called John's Gospel a "semi-philosophical interpretation of the Christian religion in biography." As Dean Inge, a British churchman, phrased it, the writer of John "idealized a historical figure." Inge's point is well taken; there is ample evidence that the writer tried to create an ideal Jesus, not reconstruct the real one. For example, the writer used figures of speech to define Jesus. He made Jesus say, "I am the bread of life," "I am the light of the world," and "I am the vine, you are the branches." These appealing figures of speech denote a very real unity between Jesus and his disciples, but they also denote an other-worldly figure. Further proof of this tendency can be seen when the writer depicts Jesus as a figure entering the life of the world, walking on water, or turning water into wine.

Perhaps because of its other-worldly quality, John's Gospel has been the source of much appealing devotional reading. The words from the fourteenth and fifteenth chapters have given great comfort to the sorrowing. They reassure people facing death, "Let not your heart be troubled; you believe, believe also in me. In my Father's house are many mansions . . . .I go to prepare a place for you . . .that where I am, you may be also." John's vision of Jesus offers a complement to the vision contained in the synoptic Gospels —quite incomplete in itself, but a facet of Christianity we would not want to lose.

Jesus in the Letter of John

There are other interpretations of Jesus present in the three short letters, sometimes called Epistles, that follow the Gospel section of the New Testament. These letters sharply delineate theological differences that have marked religious movements up to the present day. The Epistles are attributed to John. But which John? No one knows with certainty, but we do know that they were written around the first part of the second century A.D. The letters are appealing. They have something of the quality of Paul's epistles on love, found in the thirteenth chapter of his first letter to the Corinthians.

The writer of the letters speaks like a fatherly or a grandfatherly figure. He addresses his readers as "My little children." He says that his reason for writing is "so that you may not sin, but if one does sin, we have an advocate with the Father, Jesus Christ the righteous, and he is the expiation for our sins, and not for our sins only but also for the sins of the whole world." The writer also speaks of "walking in the light as God is in the light, having fellowship with one another, while the blood of Jesus Christ cleanses us from all sin."

This second letter of John makes love the dominant motive, the ruler of the faithful life, stating that "there is no fear in love, but perfect love casteth out fear." Moreover, if you say, "I love God," but hate your brother, you are a liar, "for he who does not love his brother whom he has seen, cannot love God whom he has not seen. And this is the commandment we have from him, that he who loved God should love his brother also."

On this appeal to an all-encompassing love, John grounds his faith that Jesus is the Son of the Father. John contends that anyone who believes that Jesus is the Son of God, that He is the Christ, is himself a child of God. He leaves no room for doubt on that score when he pointedly questions, "Who is the liar but he who denies the Father *and* the Son? This is the anti-Christ, he who denies the Father and the Son. No one who denies the Son has the Father. He who confesses the Son has the Father also."

What does John, or the writer of these letters, mean by these repeated and emphatic statements? The text reads as if he is carrying on an argument with someone, and in all likelihood he was. Some newcomers to the Church had probably brought with them views that the writer considered dangerous to the life of the Church. Perhaps they were members of the group who called themselves Docetists ("seemists"). Influenced by a philosophy that held that all the material world was evil, and that only the Spirit was good, the Docetists claimed that God (who was good) could not inhabit flesh (which was evil). Therefore, they reasoned, God could not really have been in Jesus—it only "seemed" that way. The John of these letters represented the mainstream philosophy, which asserted that God *had* descended into the evil world, abasing Himself in order to redeem humanity. John presents his case so strongly that it has become the theology of Orthodox Christianity to the present day. He also gains support from Paul, who reaffirmed this theology when he declared, "God was in Christ, reconciling the world unto himself." But it remained for John to forcefully set matters straight. He asserted that Christ was the Son of the Father, saying, "The love of God [was] made manifest among us, that God sent his only Son into the world, that through him we might find the way of love and salvation."

Significantly, in his letters John says nothing about the *human* Jesus—the dynamic Jesus who visited in the homes of friends and foes, who argued upon the highways with legalists and self-righteous scribes, and who became so deeply involved with the questions, problems, and sufferings of his society. Jesus' commitment to earthly life is irrelevant to John. For him Jesus possesses a transcendent nature—he is God's Son, sent to earth to express God's love for man. To the last, John contends that the only meaningful test of faith, love and forgiveness is whether one accepts Jesus as Christ.

The use of the term *Christ*—from the Greek—reveals that John was not talking about Jesus as the Jewish Messiah, but as a transcendent spirit of God who lived in the hearts of believers. This concept of Jesus has been one of the strongest influences in the life of the Church, and a dominant view in traditional Christian theology. It has also, alas, been the source of most of Christianity's most bloody heresies, for it establishes a logical contradiction that has tempted some of the greatest minds to try to find a solution. For some, faith has not been enough.

The Book of Hebrews

This shift in outlook reflected in John's letters leads to a second problem, faced in Hebrews. Was Jesus a sacrifice for the sins of the world? This has been one of the most widely held doctrines of the Christian Churches. It has been expressed—as I indicated in an early chapter—in many songs and hymns. Often the doctrine puts great stress upon the actual blood of Christ.

I recall some years ago visiting a church in Bruges, Belgium. It was called the "Church of the Holy Blood," because it claimed to have a few of the drops caught at Calvary. This blood had been preserved in a small vial which was guarded as a holy relic. The church attributed special powers to this bit of blood from Jesus' body. People came to church bringing all kinds of objects (such as handkerchiefs and beads) to be blessed. It is often surprising how legends and fictions recur—such people have returned full circle to the primitive animism of the early Hebrews, who felt Yahweh's presence in the Ark gave them miraculous powers.

In another instance of a return to earlier patterns, the Book of Hebrews seems to make Jesus a sacrifice similar to those the ancient Hebrew people had made on the altar. In the Catholic Church this doctrine reaches a more sophisticated expression, but it has something of the same significance.

Except for one chapter, Hebrews is a book that is relatively unknown. The exception is the eleventh chapter, in which there is a roll call of the great heroes of both the Old and New Testaments. Like the Book of Revelation, which will be discussed in its own chapter, Hebrews was written at a time of persecution. Unlike Revelation, however, the writer of Hebrews was concerned specifically with the conditions existing during the later persecutions. His intention was similar to that of Daniel's author: to offer solace to his unhappy people, and to encourage them to persevere.

The writer of Hebrews urged his people not to neglect the great salvation which had been offered to them. He summed up this great salvation as "the perfect sacrifice"—a sacrifice offered by a perfect priest. He assured his readers that Jesus was the perfect offering for the sins of the world, saying,

> Therefore, brethren, since we have confidence to enter the sanctuary by the blood of Jesus, by the new and living way . . .and since we have a great priest over the house of God . . .let us hold fast the confession of our hope without wavering . . .and let us consider how to stir up one another in good works, not neglecting to meet together, as is the habit of some, but encouraging one another, and all the more as you see the Day drawing near.

The ideas and words of this book are often used to confirm the faith held by some that salvation comes directly from the sacrifice of Christ, and that man's sin was so great that only a perfect sacrifice could suffice.

Here, then, are the scriptural references which have given rise to the differing movements and denominations of Christianity. Our study thus far shows how difficult it is for adherents of any one view to claim the support of that infallible book, the Bible. It also makes clear how impossible it is to recognize with absolute certainty *the* historic Jesus. What we read in the New Testament is a succession of interpretations of Jesus—interpretations made long after his life in an attempt to recapture the experience that changed our world.

The most thorough modern study made in the effort of discovering what Jesus was like was that of the great missionary doctor, theologian and musician Albert Schweitzer. He describes his search through all the sources available in his book *The Quest for the Historic Jesus*. While Schweitzer acknowledges the impossibility of ever knowing the historical Jesus, he finally expresses the following masterful truth about all our quests:

> We find no designation which expressed what He is for us. He comes to us as One unknown, without a name, as of old, by the lakeside, He came to those men who knew Him not. He speaks to us the same word; "follow thou me" and sets us to the tasks He has to fulfill for our time. He commands, and to those who obey Him, whether they be wise or simple, He will reveal Himself in the toils, the conflicts, the sufferings which they shall pass through in His fellowship, and, as an ineffable mystery, they shall learn in their own experience Who He Is.[14]

A Modern Search

The conclusion quoted above from the writings of Dr. Albert Schweitzer is generally accepted by biblical scholars today. They recognize that a more adequate knowledge of the historic Jesus was not attempted by the writers of the

Gospels and the Epistles. These writers were not writing biographies of Jesus; they were writing interpretations of Jesus in the light of the theologies that had developed in the decades after the death of Jesus.

By the time the New Testament was written, Jesus had become a transcendent figure. Many miraculous stories had developed around his memory. Most would concede that without these stories which were incorporated into the records there would have been no Christian Church as we have known it in history. These stories, and the theological interpretations about Jesus' birth, death, and Resurrection, have furnished the mystery and drama supporting the dogmas and the worship of the Church.

Similar observations could be made about all religions. No religion is unique in the matter of stories and myths. All religions deal with man's wonders about the unknown and the mysterious. Faith is what we believe about what we don't know, and it is best sustained by stories and myths.

The stories about Jesus, along with the theories to explain God's plan of salvation, have thus been more powerful in holding the allegiance of the people of the Christian churches than a more complete record of the daily activities of Jesus might have accomplished.

Granting the above observation, it is still important to realize that the ethical standards and moral values needed to create healthy and sensitive societies and nations are transmitted more powerfully by the example of historic persons who have exhibited sacrificial love and concern for others. This calls for a greater appreciation of the human Jesus.

Of course, it cannot be charged that the loving concern of Jesus for the people of his day has been overlooked in biblical records. It is evident, however, that the emphasis of the Church over the centuries on the supernatural nature of Jesus, and on the miraculous elements of his life, has overshadowed the full dimensions of his humanity and the depth of his concerns. Certainly it was true that often the leaders of the Church were so concerned with their own spiritual power over the lives of their people and with dealing with heresy that they failed to express the sympathetic grace of the Man of Nazareth.

As the result of many historic forces, there is much that we do not know about the daily life of Jesus and the problems he faced. This lack of knowledge caused G. Studdert-Kennedy, the much loved chaplain of the British forces in World War I, to lament:

> I wonder what he charged for chairs at Nazareth?
> And did they cheat him so, and beat him down,
> And brag about it 'round the town: "I bought it
> Cheap for half a crown from that mad carpenter?"

There are other questions we would like to ask. How did Jesus make his living after he left his father's carpenter shop? Was his mother concerned about her son's future when she went out to hear him preach one day (as recorded in Mark)? Was she beginning to worry about his associations with his radical cousin, John the Baptist? John was in trouble with Herod the King. And there were others in the group under suspicion. Two brothers, disciples of Jesus, were known to be Zealots. The Romans were suspicious of them. When crowds came to hear Jesus, his group disturbed the authorities. They said the group was "possessed of demons." They were seen as troublemakers.

In years to come Jesus was to be called "The Son of God," and members of his feared group were to be made Saints by the Church. Peter, impulsive as he was, was to be given, according to popular legend, the keys to the kingdom of heaven. But now we look back and ask questions.

How did the little group survive? Did they form a commune, much as groups do today? Did they sleep by the side of the road, or did friends take them in? Jesus said of himself, "The foxes have holes, and the birds of the air have nests, but the Son of Man hath nowhere to lay his head."

In the light of the above questions, what was the significance of the advice Jesus gave to the rich young man to "sell all that you have and give to the poor, and come follow me"? Such advice still disturbs members of Christian churches when they read or hear some of the radical teachings of Jesus in his much quoted Sermon on the Mount. The questions are growing. How can we translate into the culture and organized structure of modern society, with its manifold problems, the seemingly simple ethics of Jesus?

It seems now, in the light of the studies of Dr. Schweitzer and others, that we shall never know much of the personal life of Jesus. It was, however, the hope of many that, with the increased knowledge now available concerning the writing of the Gospels, the readers of the Bible might have more insight into the fuller dimensions of Jesus' human interests. The human and humane concerns of Jesus might give insight into the vast problems that present societies and nations face. Such seemed to be the hope of a writer whose name I have forgotten but whose words stay with me, who in a critical study of the Bible wrote:

> If darkness ever comes upon the earth and every human virtue grows dim, then it is that the personality of Jesus will save us.

During the latter part of the past century and the early years of the present, a movement developed known as the Modernist Movement. This movement was based upon critical research of the Bible over the past several centuries —possibly starting after the French Revolution, a time when all authority, religious as well as civil, was being questioned.

The introduction of the Modernist Movement into American religious life led to controversies in theological seminaries and in churches. In the seminaries, some eminent scholars lost their teaching posts. A long battle began between those who followed the finding of the scholars mentioned above and those who held to the belief in the literal accuracy of the Bible. The latter were known as Fundamentalists.

The Fundamentalist–Modernist controversy of the twenties and thirties of this century centered largely around Dr.

Harry Emerson Fosdick. Dr. Fosdick, a Baptist minister, was a brilliant preacher and teacher at Union Theological Seminary in New York. In his book, *The Man From Nazareth,* Dr. Fosdick reexamines the problem confronted by Dr. Schweitzer. While agreeing essentially with Dr. Schweitzer that we cannot know the historic Jesus, Dr. Fosdick points out that the critical reader of the Gospels can see and understand much of what Jesus was like through the eyes of his contemporaries. He suggests that we "put ourselves in the place of the outcastes and sinners, the women and children, the patriotic nationalists, as well as Jesus' disciples." Of these persons, he writes, "there is a vast amount of information, both in the New Testament and outside it, concerning such groups, their prejudices and convictions, their personal and social needs." "What if," continues Dr. Fosdick, "we should start with these, identify ourselves with their attitudes, we might at least see Jesus as they saw him, and, in the end, compose a composite picture of him, as these folk, friendly and hostile, looked at him."[15]

At present, one of the strongest supporters of stressing the importance of the historic Jesus is the distinguished Catholic theologian Father Hans Kung. He has been teaching for two decades at West Germany's Tubingen University. In his book *On Being a Christian*, described by Brian O. McDermott in the May 1980 *Atlantic,* Father Kung "builds a case for Christianity as a religion of Radical Humanism." McDermott continues, "Because Jesus is the radically human person, because he was so thoroughly identified with God's cause and ours, Christians can find in him the power and pattern for their own lives."

Thus we find Jesus of Nazareth an ever challenging figure —interpreted by people of all ages in the context of the felt need of that age.

The next chapter deals with the first great series of tests of the early Christians in their contest with the State—which has often felt imperiled by the needs of people such as those discerned by the disciples of Jesus.

15

Hope for the Persecuted

We have only one book in the Bible left to discuss, perhaps the most needed one today. The Book of Revelation has great symbolic relevance for today's reader. The obvious historic parallels between biblical times and those of today are not easily shrugged off—nor should they be—for the Bible is meant to be learned from, to be *read*.

Revelation was written by a man of the period A.D. 81–96 who called himself John. John stated that he wrote from the Isle of Patmos; his writings were directed to the Seven Christian Churches of Asia, which were suffering persecution at the hands of Emperor Domitian. The purpose of John's writings was to predict events which were shortly to come to pass—predictions that would bring the hope of release to the members of these churches.

As we have seen, the early decades of the Christian Churches were years of turmoil. Then as now new movements were viewed as threats. People saw them as dangerous innovations, and their efforts to suppress each one sound a familiar note today. Threats, intimidations, violence, and even death were all techniques of suppression employed by the Romans. We have seen how Paul faced the hostility of Jewish opponents who formed mobs to disrupt his meetings. These agent provocateurs fomented angry demonstrations, creating disruptions that would lead to charges of civil disorder against Paul. Like more modern martyrs,

Paul suffered imprisonment, abuse, and (as tradition has it) finally death at the hands of the Roman authorities.

The Roman government, which shared at least something of the Hellenic feeling of universalism, was not greatly concerned with minor squabbles between Paul and elements of the Jewish communities. But authority breeds responsibility, and Rome was committed to keeping order among its subject peoples. Charges of disloyalty, such as those levied against Paul, were a politic and convenient cause for alarm.

We can understand the nature of Rome's problem if we consider how vigorously the government of the United States, like most other contemporary governments, has pursued those who are accused of disloyalty. In the early fifties, writers and actors were blacklisted for the merest hint of association with communists. In the late sixties, American youth protesting the war in Vietnam were jailed or driven to other countries to escape prosecution because they refused to serve in the armed forces. Still others were harassed for their radical criticism of the free enterprise system, and they too were sometimes charged with conspiring against the government.

Like the Vietnam War protestors, the early Christians refused to serve in the armed forces. Influenced by the love ethic of Jesus and Paul, they sought to love their enemies, to do good to those who despitefully used them, and to dedicate their lives to reconciliation. Such attitudes, held by the people of any nation, appear to threaten the authority and power of government, and it has become traditional to charge such nonconformists with treason. The early Christians' refusal to serve in the armed forces was founded on a deeper, more directly subversive basis—they refused to accept the Emperor as a divine king. But the Emperor regarded himself as divine and demanded ritual observance from his subjects. This the Christians refused to give him. Instead, they insisted on publicly worshipping the God who Jesus had made known to them.

The recalcitrant attitude of the early Christians made them easy scapegoats for any trouble or disaster that came upon the country. According to Tacitus, Nero (the Emperor who set fire to Rome) sought to divert the blame for widespread unrest and dissatisfaction with his government to the Christians (just as President Nixon did by lumping together drugs, crime, and anti-war protest as opposed to the banner of "law and order"). Nero, under the influence of his wife, Poppaea (a Jewish Proselyte), charged the Christians with being publicly unpatriotic, with being atheists, and with being generally unsociable. As a result of Poppaea's charges the Roman historian Tacitus tells us, "They [the Christians] were made the subject of sport in their death, they were covered with the hides of wild beasts, worried to death by the dogs, and set on fire to serve as nocturnal lights."

In addition to standard charges of disloyalty, there were frenzied charges of abnormal behavior amongst the Christians. Whispers accused them of worshipping a donkey's head, and of eating babies (highly inflammatory charges are common weapons against the members of any movement that rejects the accepted mores of society, and typically breed a blood frenzy similar to that observed among sharks). The second charge was the more serious, for it had a basis in Christian ritual—it was doubtless inspired by reports of the Lord's Supper which Christians celebrated in secret with the formula, "This is my body broken for you. Take. Eat."

Official persecutions of the Christians occurred intermittently over many years. They came often enough, however, to keep the Christians living in constant fear. It was during one severe outbreak of terror and persecution during the reign of Emperor Domitian (A.D. 81–96) that the Book of Revelation appeared. The writer of this book addressed himself to the Seven Churches of Asia and offered hope when there seemed to be none. He promised a final victory for Christendom, and immediate redemption for Christians who remained loyal to their faith. Grasping for hope in their desperation, suffering Christians welcomed the picturesque language that depicted how the deliverance would come. The writer, John, was accepted as a prophet.

In writing to the members of these churches, John expressed his profound sorrow. He was displeased to see their unfaithfulness. He upbraided some of the churches for their failure, saying that they had weakly given way before the fierceness of the persecution (a factor which history records caused much contention after the persecution abated). There were, however, some churches which John praised highly for their good works and their heroism. But to all of them he urged patience and perseverance; they had only to await the triumphant end that was soon to come.

The Book of Revelation is similar in many respects to the Book of Daniel, which we discussed in Chapter 8. There are, however, several major differences. While the writer of the Book of Daniel was dealing with events that had already taken place, the writer of the Book of Revelation dealt with events transpiring at the very time of the writing; where the writer of Daniel used fiction and analogy to inspire hope in the lives of the people of Jerusalem in the year 165 B.C., John made precise predictions of things which would soon happen, such as the death of the Emperor and the fall of the Roman Empire.

Admittedly, John did not speak directly of the fall of Rome—he used the word Babylon—but this was the language of the oppressed. For example, when he substituted a pejorative title, the Beast, for the Roman Emperor, his readers knew whom he meant. His message of hope sustained the Christians through their ordeals, while it fooled the Romans.

John went on to predict that the Lord would appear, bind Satan, and hold him for a thousand years. At the end of that time (what he called the Millennium), Satan would be released, and he would gather up the forces of evil to lead them into a final battle for control of the world. In the end, John promised, a warrior on a white horse would appear to lead the forces of righteousness in the battle of Armageddon. This new army of heaven would, he continued, defeat the devil and set up God's kingdom, a kingdom of righteousness that would endure forever.

In unforgettable language, John described the new heaven and new earth that God would create. Earthly cares would pass away, and in the new realm there would be no tears and no death. To those who had endured to the end, a "crown of life" would be given. As for those who had not kept faith, a burning lake of fire awaited them all.

This glorious picture of a new age set in classic form the hopes that religious groups in every age have envisioned as the end of their struggle. Persecuted by religious tyranny or oppressed by injustices and despairing of any release save through divine intervention, such groups have tied their hopes to the spectacular rewards offered by the Book of Revelation. They deplore the evils they endure, but they hope for deliverance. They take quite literally the final picture in Revelation, and look forward with eager promise to this last battle in which the forces of righteousness will triumph.

The hope expressed in the Book of Revelation has been a recurring one. People of every succeeding age have used the books of Daniel and Revelation to buttress their hope. They have interpreted the symbolic words of these books to refer to conditions in their own time. John's condemnation of the Beast, for instance, was interpreted as pointing to the Mohammedans when Europe was threatened by Moorish invasion. In the Middle Ages the dubious title was applied by early Protestants to the Pope; in the eighteenth century it was given to Napoleon. This century has seen it used to describe first the Kaiser, then Hitler. You can be sure that history will provide new examples; for the Beast is a constant threat.

Some of the most dynamic religious leaders of our own time are convinced that the world is getting worse, that we are headed for destruction. Like their forebears, they rest their hope for the future on the promises made in the Book of Revelation. Revelation provides a fitting conclusion to the Bible, as if these teachers of our past were telling us, "Yes, you have learned much. But there comes a time when your learning will be severely tested. When that day comes, do not despair. When the seven trumpets blow, you will cross the great divide."

Conclusion

You have now read my thoughts and the product of my research about the nature of the books of the Bible. Some of the books have not been mentioned, others have been dealt with only briefly. None of them has been completely examined especially with regard to its logical contents. That was not my intention in writing this book. What I did set out to do was to introduce you, in a comparatively simple and brief book, to something of the nature of the Bible, that you might know how the various books came to be written, what the purpose of the writers was, and what their sources were.

A friend of mine who practices law gave me a useful analogy to my endeavor while speaking about the nature of legal problems. He said that in law, the basic starting point for the construction of any writing (deed, contract, or will) is that "it must be read in the circumstances of its formulation." Then, turning to the problem of biblical interpretation, he said that our troubles with the Bible have stemmed from our failure to realize this basic fact. I believe that what I have written in this approach to biblical writings will satisfy even the lawyers among you.

My explanation of the background of the writings in the Bible should assist you in clarifying some of the more contradictory and imaginative material recorded in the Scriptures. For those of you desiring a larger knowledge of the Bible, I have listed in the bibliography a number of books and commentaries that should be helpful in further pursuing the ideas I express in this book. These books are available in most good libraries.

Ultimately, I have only touched on the full meaning of the Bible, for the Bible deals with the whole range of life's experiences. Some of its writings are narrowly concerned with laws that regulated the lives of people in an ancient time and have no application whatsoever to modern circumstances. But most of its writings transcend the time of their publication. These include passages of rare devotional expressions that voice praise and thanksgiving in unforgettably beautiful prose. Ironically, some of these tender and beautiful expressions of devotion to God are set in the context of narrow racial and national concerns. Nevertheless, the Bible contains many models of ethical thought which we must follow if we are to survive and flourish. In the final analysis, the Bible is more than a history, more than a compilation of interesting folklore, and more than a bone of theological contention—it is a landmark of inspiration.

Yet there is a danger that our biblical heritage will slip away, that through sloth, internecine squabbles, or rigid sectarianism we will smother our desire to understand the Bible. If this happens, we will lose much of the meaning of our poetry, music and art—not to mention the religions that justify all these endeavors.

Biblical inquiry and study serve a vital function today. We need to keep alive the idealism, the sense of moral struggle, and the realism that are preeminent in the Bible's writings. Why do we need such inquiry? Struggling to be born on earth is a cooperative world culture—a culture whose realization depends upon something of the universalism of the Hebrew prophets and the understanding love and insights of Jesus of Nazareth. Will you join the struggle?

Appendix

In his book *God and the Social Process,* Graham Wallis throws additional light upon the reasons behind some of the supposedly prehistoric stories. He wrote:

> An important consideration to bear in mind is that the development of the nation in Palestine gives a pattern, or ground rule, whereon are woven the striking Hebrew legends about earlier ages, before the dawn of written history. Instead of being merely unsubstantiated... these legends prove to be of significance in relation to events recorded in the books of Judges, Samuel and Kings, and the prophets....

The above thesis written by Dr. Wallis is illustrated in several well-known stories in Genesis. It is thought, for instance, that the story of the murder of Abel by Cain (Genesis 4) was introduced into the narrative of the J writers at a much later time to explain the hostility that had erupted between the herdsmen of the hill and the agricultural workers of the valleys.

Also, there is the story of Noah, who was saved from the Flood, and later found drunk by his son Ham. Noah, according to the narrative in the ninth chapter of Genesis, cursed Ham and doomed him and his descendants to lives as servants forever. This story is thought to explain the Hebrews' enslavement of the Canaanites (descended from Ham).

Likewise, the story of Jacob's treachery in securing the birthright of his brother Esau was introduced (according to Wallis' interpretation) to justify Israel's right to tribute from the Edomites. The Israelites did not consider the

Edomites worthy of freedom. Esau, the forefather of the Edomites, had sold his birthright.

As Graham Wallis states it (page 47 of the book referred to above):

> The documents which finally become the Bible were prepared by many different writers who lived at various places in successive ages, when there was no sense of history, and none of our modern feeling of literary property, so that a scribe—who compiled a roll of writing out of earlier documents and folk tales —felt free to interpret comments and make additions.

Notes

1. Benedict De Spinoza. *A Theological Political Treatise* (Dover Publishing Co., 1951).

2. Mary Howard. Review of *The Strange Silence of the Bible in the Church* by James D. Smart. Union Seminary Quarterly.

3. *Autobiography of Mark Twain,* edited by Charles Nelder. (Harper's, 1950), p. 5.

4. Ibid., p. 5.

5. Arnold Toynbee. *A Study of History* (Oxford University Press, 1940), p. 44.

6. James Moffatt. *Translation of the Bible* (Introduction) (Hodder and Stoughton, 1924), p. xii.

7. Harvey Cox. *Seduction of the Spirit* (Simon and Schuster), p. 9.

8. Graham Wallis. *God and the Social Process* (University of Chicago Press, 1935), p. 15.

9. Fleming James. *Personalities of the Old Testament.*

10. Harry Gersh. *The Sacred Books of the Jews* (Stern and Day, 1968), p. 145.

11. Herbert Willets. *Abingdon Commentary,* (Abingdon Press, 1975), p. 746.

12. Shirley Case. *Highways of Christian Doctrine* (Willet Clark and Co., 1936), p. 8–9.

13. Joseph Klausner. *Jesus, His Life and Teachings* (Macmillan and Co.), p. 197.

14. Albert Schweitzer. *The Quest for the Historic Jesus.* (Macmillan and Co., 1948), p. 401.

15. Harry E. Fosdick. *The Man From Nazareth.* (Harper and Bro., 1949).

Bibliography

Abingdon Bible Commentary. Nashville: Abingdon Press, 1975. (A one-volume commentary on the Bible.)

Buck, Pearl S. *The Story Bibb*. The Bartholomew House, 1971. (Simply written story following the traditional order of the writings.)

Goodspeed, Edgar J. *The Story of the Bible*. University of Chicago Press, 1936. (A brief summary of the books of the Bible.)

Grey, Robert Munson. *I Yahweh*. Willet Clark & Co., 1937. (A fanciful imaginative autobiography of Yahweh, a novel in the form of an autobiography.)

Interpreter's Bible Series. 12 Volume Commentary. Nashville: Abingdon Press, 1951–1957 (Volume 1 contains valuable articles on Old Testament history.)

Phillips, J.B. *Letters To The Young Churches*. New York: Macmillan Co., 1957. (A modern translation of the New Testament Epistles.)

Sandmel, Samuel. *The Hebrew Scriptures*. New York: Knopf, 1963. (An introduction to the literature and ideas of the Jewish people.)

Toynbee, Arnold, Editor. *The Crucible of Christianity*. New York: World Publishing Co., 1969. (An analysis of Judaism, Hellenism, and the historical background to the Christian faith.)